AF471147

Yesterday's Yesteryears

Lesney 'Matchbox' Models

**Robert Carter
& Eddy Rubinstein**

Foulis

Haynes

First published 1986

A FOULIS Book

Published by:
Haynes Publishing Group
Sparkford, Yeovil, Somerset BA22 7JJ.
England

Haynes Publications Inc.
861 Lawrence Drive, Newbury Park,
California 91320 USA

British Library Cataloguing in Publication Data

Carter, Robert J.
   Yesterday's yesteryears.
   1. Matchbox toys—Collectors and collecting
   I. Title   II. Rubinstein, Eddy
   688.7'2   TS2301.T7

ISBN 0-85429-578-X

Library of Congress catalogue card number
   86-82631

Editor: Robert Iles
Page layout: Mike King
Printed in England by:
J.H. Haynes & Co. Ltd.

MODELS OF YESTERYEAR
No 4
No 4
SERIES
BY LESNEY
REGD.
MADE IN ENGLAND
SHAND MASON
HORSE DRAWN FIRE ENGINE
Y-4
New Model
"MATCHBOX"
MARCA REGISTRADA
REGD. U.S. PAT. OFF.
"MODELS OF YESTERYEAR"
HORSE DRAWN FIRE ENGINE
Y-4
Y-4
MADE IN ENGLAND
"MATCHBOX" REGD T.M. G.B. AND ABROAD
A LESNEY PRODUCT
HORSE DRAWN
FIRE ENGINE
Y-4

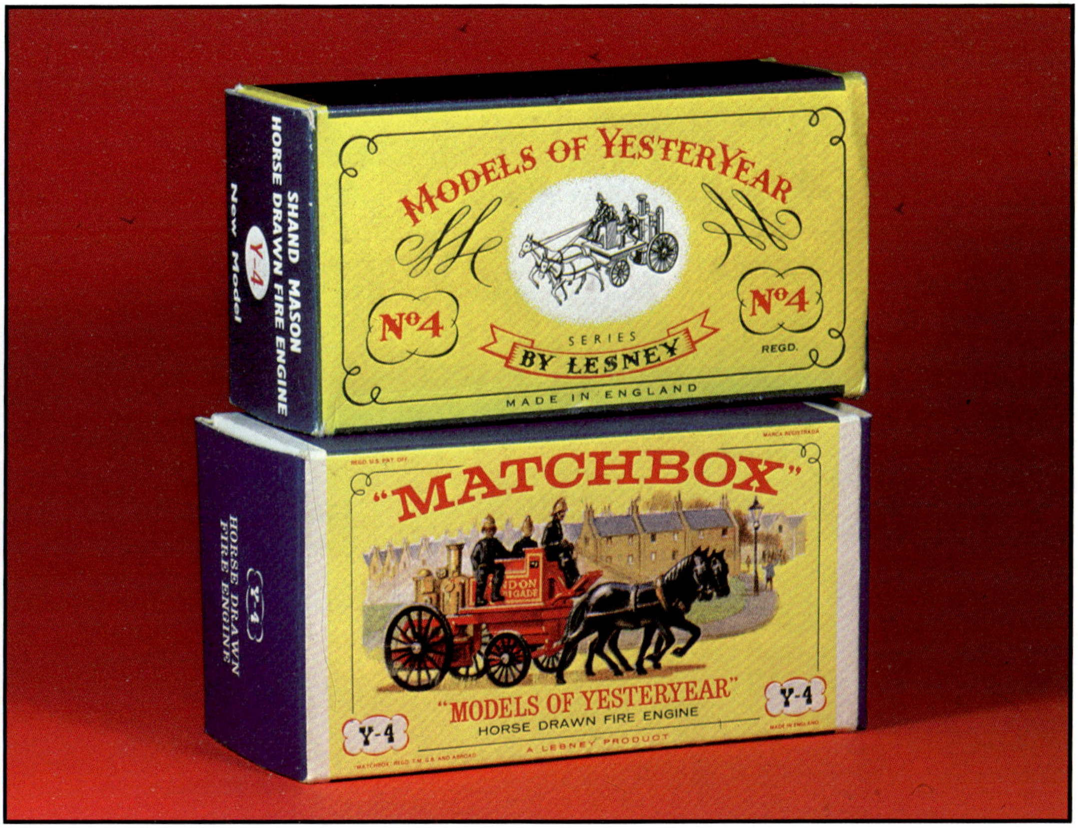

Yesterday's Yesteryears

Introduction

Since the collection of die-cast model vehicles has become such a widespread hobby to both young and old alike, perhaps more so to the 'grown-up' collectors who so eagerly await each new release and spend so much time and money (particularly the latter) in the pursuit of the rare or the near unobtainable, the market has generated a wealth of literature devoted to the cataloguing and pricing of such models, or toys as they should in many cases more correctly be called.

The many different makes of model on sale, and within those makes so many subjects for collection, means that for anybody specialising in any particular item such as commercial, racing or farmyard to name but three widely contrasting examples, information on any one subject is usually confined to a few chapters in a work of reference dealing with the hobby as a whole. Very few makes, series or classes have enjoyed the luxury of a guide to themselves until quite recent times, and these have tended to concentrate on the manufacturer's whole output rather than any of his individual series.

This book, as its title implies, focuses on the toys produced since the 1950s under the Lesney label "Models of Yesteryear" for the simple reason that the compilers, keen collectors themselves, reluctantly concluded that the sort of book they were actually looking for did not then exist.

Some very good ones did exist which contributed quite a lot to the hobby in their own fields. The 'specialist' price guides for example, meticulously up-dated as they sometimes are, provide not only an

excellent basis for discussion and barter when the models change hands, but reasonably well detailed descriptions of the products which are invaluable to anybody trying to build up a collection of their own. With one or two exceptions however, they tend to be rather sparsely illustrated. A greater attention to detail is a feature of the listings which, ignoring the possible cost of the items they describe, present facets of such infinite variation that though they might be essential to those whose collecting enthusiasm borders on the fanatic, the reader can become hopelessly lost in a welter of 'as before but with's. These however tend to be even less illustrated than the price guides.

Firm believers in the old adage that one picture is worth a thousand words, the compilers of this simple guide hope that by showing the models in their more-or-less basic colours it will fall somewhere between the confusingly too descriptive and/or partially illustrated publications and those which, though profusely and in some cases beautifully illustrated, embrace a wide range of makes and periods including those which are less likely to appeal to the die-cast vintage vehicle enthusiast, thus enabling such individuals to build up their basic collections and at the same time learn about the subtler variations as those collections progress.

If we can eliminate from the 'Swapmeet' scene the occasional startled cry of "Good grief, I didn't know they did *that* one in *pink*" we shall have succeeded.

London, September 1984
R. J. C/E. A. R.

Acknowledgements

We wish to express our sincere thanks and appreciation to all those who were in one way or another involved in the preparation of this book, in particular to Mr. Les Duplock of Model Road and Rail who very sportingly lent us the models not available from our own collections. Our thanks are also due to the many stall holders at the Swapmeets and Toy Fairs we attend, with whom it is always a pleasure to stop for a chat and who have drawn our attention to some of the subtler variations. Thanks also to an elderly father who has obligingly emigrated to less hectic locations when the more intense photographic sessions have loomed on the horizon. "Lesney", "Matchbox" and "Models of Yesteryear" are the registered trade marks of the Matchbox Group of Companies.

Robert J. Carter

To his friends 'Bob', by trade an aeronautical engineer, has apart from a brief spell in the motor trade, been in the aircraft industry all of his professional career. Veteran motorcar and aircraft enthusiast, Bob is also the sleeping (literally) partner in a modestly successful photographic agency. When awake (rarely), enjoys drinking real ale, decent beer as he calls it, motoring in his elderly (geriatric) motorcar, and visiting swapmeets and aircraft displays around the country and occasionally abroad. The only real reason that Bob has not obtained the few items missing from his collection is that they have never been on sale at that particular venue-of-the-day, located next to the pub selling the best beer.

Eddy A. Rubinstein

Anglo Swiss computer expert and aviation photographer/journalist. Eager beaver – what in the aircraft industry is usually described as a 'jet-propelled ferret'. Spends most of working time between Switzerland and England, most of leisure time between England and Switzerland trying to encourage pub fruit machines to pay for lunch (frequently successfully). Keen collector of 'Models of Yesteryear', more recently dedicated collector of 'Days Gone' which proliferate like hyper-active mice round Swiss flat and ensure that luggage carrying end of Mercedes two-seater scrapes along most of road between Richmond and Basel. Relaxes at Rhineland *Weinfests* (see photo ?) and claims to like sailing.

Chapter One

Reflections on the Yesteryear scene

It must have been an inspired moment when Matchbox toy makers Jack Odell and Leslie Smith decided to market a series of toys consisting of old-fashioned motor cars, lorries, public service vehicles, steam engines and locomotives in the mid 1950s because the range which emerged, under the title 'Models of Yesteryear', seems to have captured the imagination of the collector's world in a manner out of all proportion to the impact they could have been expected to make when they were produced. Small boys, the obvious market for toy road vehicles and railway engines, are notoriously keen on the newest, sleekest and fastest, and the introduction of this series based on elderly though not entirely obsolete machinery would have seemed a very optimistic gamble indeed.

Elderly though not obsolete? Well at the time Yesteryears were introduced the Bentley Drivers Club were holding Speed Trials in Belgium along the autoway to Brussels every year, old Morrises of the type which succeeded the 'bullnose' Morris Cowley (Y8) could be picked up for about £15 or so and a steam-driven lorry used to trundle through Heston

several mornings every week going about its lawful business. Steam Rollers were around until quite recent years and fairground traction engines never entirely disappeared.

So who bought Yesteryears in such quantities that a surprisingly large number of these nearly thirty-year old toys, have survived into the 1980s in every condition ranging from 'mint as manufactured' to well battered? After all, these are not exactly the sort of thing that can expect a long and undamaged life.

Perhaps one clue can be found in the fact that the contemporary 'Veteran & Vintage Magazine', itself a quality production of the 'fifties specialising in road vehicles of pre 1930 manufacture, as well as advertising these toys in its annual Christmas issue actually heralded the introduction of the Y15 Rolls-Royce Silver Ghost in an Editorial, while a later edition included a report on a visit to the Lesney factory. This is perhaps a little less uncommon now when there are so many magazines covering what are described as 'Classic' cars, several of which include a 'model' page and, so many models marketed, as opposed to the limited number of makes on sale (on the English market at least) at the time, but it does suggest that more people than just the children for whom Lesney normally catered, found these little vehicles quite appealing.

As one of our contemporaries put it 'They're the ideal thing to give the (car minded) girl friend when the supply of little glass animals runs out'.

From the dainty, if in some cases somewhat primitive, models of that first series the Yesteryears have become comparatively sophisticated. The very small scales employed initially have become a thing of the past and with the exception of the current vans and London bus, the lorries, steamers and locos gave way to motor cars alone, there being a gap of some seventeen

years between the last of the old Commercials and the first of the newer ones. The motor-cycle and sidecar combination, beautifully detailed in itself though not, one is led to believe, over popular, has never been repeated. So many people who own one purchased it because they felt they ought to since they had all the others, this being in the days before 100% dedicated collections.

Curiously enough one or two of the current '75' series of Matchbox Miniatures, notably the Ford 'A' Coupe, would, given old type wheels instead of the speed-wheels with which it is fitted, compare favourably with some of the first issue Yesteryears in size and simplicity.

To describe some of the early models as somewhat primitive is in no way to denigrate them. In terms of value for money they could not be bettered. Other die-cast metal toy makers in this country were to introduce their own ranges of vintage cars – nicely turned out little works of art in their own right and with the advantage that they were to a common scale (always a sore point with Yesteryear collectors). But their quality was reflected in their prices, and at a time when the addition of even a (pre-decimal) penny or twopence on the cost of anything would result in voices being raised in protest, a price difference of a shilling (5p), or more usually several shillings, was quite a consideration.

That these companies turned out their vintage models for a limited number of years only may perhaps result from this. Examples of these models may still be found at Swapmeets, though not in such great numbers as their Yesteryear contemporaries. They are still very pretty and still fairly pricey, but perhaps less so when costed against some of those contemporaries now.

By comparison the Continental scene was rather more polarised and it is barely an over-simplification to say that generally speaking the local die-cast metal models were superb and fiendishly expensive and the plastic ones cheap and somewhat cheerful. There were exceptions to this state of affairs, but not many.

So there we were, presented with a group of cheap but very eye-catching miniatures quite unlike anything then on the general, as opposed to the specialist and therefore expensive, market. Few old car enthusiasts could resist such things as a little green Bentley only a couple of inches long, a tiny 'Bullnose' Morris wearing a colour scheme typical of the original, a minute off-white racing Mercedes or a small but dignified Packard 'town carriage'.

Allowing for the fact that four wheels, four tyres and two axles account for ten parts, there were not more than a dozen-and-a-bit pieces to any of them. The radiators of the Bentley and Morris, and later the Spyker and Bugatti, were just a lick of gold paint even though the originals of some of these wore nickel rather than brass bright work. Axles were simply clenched at the non-headed end which was a fairly widely used method of retaining the wheels, and yet the 'dickey' seat of the Morris opened to reveal a seat and a footwell.

As time went by, the radiators joined the other bright-work to become plated metal, with the advantage that they could be cleaned with liquid brass polish (never wadding, which gives an unrealistic 'old gold' finish). Later on the plated metal gave way to plated plastic allowing much finer detail and a better if slightly over bright finish, while quite early on the clenched axles were replaced by axles riveted at each end which considerably improved their looks.

Throughout the life of the range minor differences occurred in the castings of many of the models. An additional reinforcing brace or thickened section here, a change of anchorage for the hood or canopy supports

there (the body side accommodating the pegs being cut away and the plastic seat mouldings extended to provide new ones in the same positions). Casting holes appeared in and disappeared from the baseplates frequently and core sizes, with their resulting witness marks, varied from batch to batch. To take a current and therefore readily available example, examination of the Y12 Ford 'T' van will show that the rear face of the body was originally smooth-surfaced to have the rear door outlines printed on. Later ones have those outlines engraved into the surface. Similarly, when the Y12 baseplate was utilised for the Y3 tankers, the Y12 on the undersurface was blanked out, so that a van baseplate can instantly be identified as being of pre- or post-1981 manufacture.

Also throughout the life of the range the scales of the Yesteryear items have varied considerably. While the collectors' model car world settled years ago for an international scale of 1:43 for die-cast and plastic model cars (as opposed to 1:32 for the early plastic kit cars) Lesney maintained a rugged, many would say obstinate, independence of their own, with scales ranging from 1:130 to 1:50, later increased to 1:35. In the early stages this becomes more readily understandable if one appreciates that their success was largely founded on their distinctive method of packing their toys. This was based on the use of boxes designed in imitation of the standard box of household matches to appeal both to children and to parents who took the view that any toy small enough to come out of a matchbox would not be expensive, hence the Lesney Matchbox label. Somehow the more sinister aspects of a combination of children and matchboxes, which would these days give some cause for concern, had remarkably little significance in what must now seem much simpler times. It is not without interest to note that the matchbox was eventually replaced for both 75

14

series and Yesteryears by 'bubble packs' and boxes as unlike the old packs as it is possible to imagine.

To be fair, it would be unrealistic to expect the employment of the same scale for models of vehicles so widely differing in size as small cars and large locomotives but at least some of the groups within the range were reasonably compatible e.g. three lorries and two buses at 1:100 and three steam traction engines at 1:180, but the situation did give rise to what must have been one of the most irritating explanations ever given, by a Lesney PRO of the time. "We're geared to the matchbox, and the scale to which we make a model depends *not on whether its owner wants to park it alongside one of our king-size dump trucks* but on whether it'll go into one of our Lesney Matchboxes". Frankly it is difficult to imagine anything in the Yesteryear range that one would *want* to park beside the aforementioned dump truck. Anyway, there seemed to be several sizes of matchbox at any given time suggesting that scale was not really considered as a significant factor, an approach which resulted in such anomalies as the 1911 Maxwell at 1:49 differing so slightly from it's Cadillac, Stutz and Thomas contemporaries at 1:48. At one time this latter looked like becoming the standard for the range when several consecutive models were released to that scale in succession.

One final thing which should be mentioned while on the subject of scales is that the variations permitted a degree of interchangeability between components such as brake/gear levers, hoods and seats which, while very useful from the production point of view also allowed some colour combinations to be found at Swapmeets and Toy Fairs which never saw the light at the Hackney factory.

The other aspect of the Yesteryear models which caused many a raised eyebrow is that of colour, which is the primary subject of this guide. In the beginning

the colours were quite realistic – everyone knew that Bentleys were green and Mercedes were white and that was all there was to it. True the Rolls-Royce Silver Ghost was added to the range in light metallic green, but most people were so impressed with the model that they didn't argue too much at the time. Then they turned out a Mercer Raceabout in *metallic lilac*. For what it is worth, Raceabouts left the Mercer factory in one of only four standard colour schemes, in which the coach striping played a major part – yellow with black stripes and blue with white stripes are two which spring to mind. Suffice it to say that metallic lilac with no stripes at all did *not* appear in the Mercer catalogue.

That said, what a delightful little model of a legendary, if fragile, motor car it was.

With the introduction of the lilac Mercer, Lesneys went into what is sometimes referred to as their 'Technicolour' or 'Disney' period which, while not embracing every model in the range – the Bugatti, Opel and Ford 'T' being notable exceptions – certainly seemed to result in at least one issue of each car produced in more than one colour turning up in the most startling, if striking, metallic colour scheme imaginable. This characteristic has only died out in quite recent years when rather more authentic colours have once again become the norm. Perhaps it should be mentioned here that it is perfectly true that old cars, Veteran cars in particular, were to be found in some very odd colour schemes indeed. The remarkable 'Dutch Pink' (narrow vertical stripes of something like black and red or yellow and green) was one such, but there is no way that the violent metallic green and plastic red of the 1911 Renault (Y2), to take one of the earliest examples, can be considered as anything other than the 'infant attracter' it was intended to be, produced by a company who were after all in the business of selling toys to children.

Whether viewed as toys for children or models for collectors some of the more unrealistically coloured cars have proved surprisingly appealing, even if some of them are jokingly reputed to glow in the dark, or should be viewed with caution after a heavy night out. One great advantage enjoyed by the collector of old Yesteryears prowling round the Toy Fairs and Swapmeets is that he or she, unlike the person originally buying each new issue as it was released and being restricted to the colour tone of that particular batch, is now able to select from the many models within each colour group on sale, the tones of their choice. Some of the metallic paints were reasonably constant but others were far from being so, such as that used on the Lagonda sometimes described as metallic orange, but varying in fact from a salmon pink to what our American cousins describe as 'Candy Apple Red'.

The illustrations in the following pages are intended to present, as far as is possible, the 'main' colours in which the Yesteryear series of models were released on to the market, without trying to differentiate between the several more subtle shades of the same colour. Other colour schemes existed in the form of paint 'tryouts' and 'one-offs'. The writer recalls seeing the 1937 Cord in a blue very similar to that used on the later version of the Riley MPH, and an attractive Mercedes 540K in silver and dark metallic blue circulates around the Toy Fair scene now and then, but these are outside the scope of this book and it is unlikely that any list detailing each one that Lesney produced (and those reputedly turned out without official sanction) could be compiled if only for the reason that there are some collectors who simply enjoy reworking and repainting their aquisitions in colours of their own choosing, and without a recognised form of certification the origins of some of the models offered for sale must be considered dubious. A few, such as the famous

white Duesenberg are becoming better known while others, half seen at a crowded Toy Fair with an absurd price attached, need far more than a vendor's hand-on-heart assurance that he didn't do a quick respray or a plastic transplant job the night before.

Neither is it the intention of this guide to get involved in the pricing or rarity 'value' of the models depicted. Quite apart from the fact that one is heavily dependent on the other, there are excellent price guides on the market for this purpose. It must be remembered however that, as the producer of one of the best of them stresses, they are for guidance only and the prices asked for a specific model may vary considerably from any guide price quoted owing to many factors; even such things as the size and location of a Swapmeet can have some bearing.

There is also the consideration that however rare a model may be, nothing is unobtainable – for the right price.

On a lighter note there is the reflection that the model you spend months hunting for will turn up in profusion – cheaper – *after* you have acquired it.

A not always appreciated aspect of the collectors' world is that a higher value is placed on a collectable item if it can be presented in the original box, particularly if that box is in as crisp and pristine a condition as it was when the shopkeeper handed it over to its first purchaser. It is true that there is nothing quite like the thrill of opening up a twenty-year old, though apparently 'brand new', box and finding inside a model as bright, clean and fresh as when it was packed at the factory all those years ago. Such models are not necessarily even rare, some surviving as unsold stock from the past, others in the hands of collectors who keep their models in the boxes and the boxes out of the sunlight, though even then cardboard boxes do tend to dry out and one opened even a couple of dozen

times in half as many years will start to lose its end
flaps. However, the result of this particular idio-
syncrasy is that the price asked for a boxed model will
be higher than that asked for an unboxed one, and a
good box can represent up to about a quarter of the
asking price. In the case of an older and probably more
expensive model this can mean quite a lot of money for
an elderly cardboard box, the implication being that
the model has lived in its box all of its life and will be in
the best possible condition to the standard of quality
accepted by the manufacturer. Hence the expression
'Mint and Boxed' used to describe some models at the
point of sale.

Unfortunately, while reputable dealers can be relied
upon to supply models in this condition it is not
unknown for a purchaser to find that his 'boxed' model
has been standing on a shelf somewhere collecting dust
and grime for years while the box has been carefully
stored in better conditions than the model. Some
attractively presented boxed models have been found,
on closer examination, to have sustained paint chips
and grazes, or even quite amateurish repairs to the
plastic components, before being hastily dusted and
repacked in their boxes for resale.

This is just one of the pitfalls for the unwary. There
are others.

If one discounts the Gift Sets issued up to and
including the 'window box' period, and packed in
containers similar in style and colouring to those
housing the contemporary individually packaged
models, Yesteryear boxes came in four different types
during the 27 years under review. Among some of those
types there were a number of sub-divisions. In the
interests of simplicity it is not proposed to detail each
printing variation used for the original matchboxes,
and there were several, but this guide identifies the four
basic types below for easy recognition to identify the

appropriate boxes for the models within their own timescale. This has been included because of a recently observed tendency for some of the older models to be offered for sale in boxes inappropriate to their age, such as the original Y15 Rolls-Royce Silver Ghosts in late type boxes produced for the subsequently issued Y10 Silver Ghosts, or Y1 Ford 'T's in modern Y12 boxes.

The four types were as follows:
(1) The original 'Matchbox', yellow with blue or dark coloured sides and some of the early ends, having any one of a number of printing and pictorial layouts starting with simple line drawings and concluding with coloured pictures of the vehicle inside. Later ones had 'pictorial' ends. (MB)
(2) A 'window' box in yellow and pink, later changed to yellow and mauve, having a transparent panel at front and top and a coloured picture of the car on the back, with a simple coloured side-view on the ends. (WB)
(3) The dark brown and coloured box known as the 'Woodgrain' box, having simulated wooden ends and bottom with gold printing, a transparent panel at front and top and a coloured, rather stark, picture and description on the back. The coloured portion of the box matched, or at least complemented, the colour of the model. (WG)
(4) The 'Straw' box, in light cream with a stiffening spine supporting a box having transparent panels at front, top and rear and descriptions in three languages on the bottom. Normally decorated with gold lines, exceptions being the Harrod's Van with green lines and the 25th Anniversary van which appeared in a white box with silver lining. (STR)

Additionally, American collectors may recall that for a period of about two years around 1970 some models

were released in rather square-edged 'Bubble' packs, mounted on card backings which, in general colouring and content, matched the 'window' boxes then in general use elsewhere.

The codes (MB), (WB), (WG) or (ST) are included here for cross-reference with the models listed in the Index. The listing does not necessarily mean that each model appeared only in the boxes shown, although it is based on those in which many of the models illustrated in the guide were purchased but it does mean that no box should be more than one up or down from that listed at the very most. In nearly all cases where the model is illustrated in colour on the box the model should match the picture. Some notable exceptions to this are the red Y5 Bugattis often sold in 'blue' Bugatti boxes and the Y3 Benz models, each one of which issued in a new colour scheme invariably first turned up in the box picturing the previous version before the picture changed to suit the model.

It should here be observed that although the models are frequently referred to by their 'Y' numbers in these notes, the use of stroke (/) numbers to identify any one of several models bearing the same Y number has been avoided. Many attempts have been made to bracket Yesteryears as '1st Series', '2nd Series' et seq, but with a range of 14, then 15 progressing to 21 and later 25 models, each one of which has to have a first release, this is not very practical. The fact is that Lesneys simply re-used Y numbers when the models previously issued under those numbers ceased to be produced, resulting in the anomalous situation whereby during the life of the so-called 2nd Series the last of the 1st Series were still just available when the first of the, by now thoroughly confused 3rd Series started to reach the shops. Lesney themselves used '/' numbers internally for the identification of the first, second and subsequent models bearing the same Y number.

Anyone dismantling a Ford T van for example will find the number Y12-3 moulded into each part of this third Y12, but to the buying public they really only used '/' numbers when cataloguing the early Y5 Talbot and Y12 Ford van paint variations though had stopped doing so by the time that the Chivers and Bird's Custard versions came along. Even then they were not consistent, examples being the Menier van (the 4th Y5) appearing as both Y5/2 and Y5/4, the Colman's as Y12/1 or Y12/4 depending on the year and destination of the catalogue. The further reflection that there is an awful lot of Y12-3 in a Y3-4 (presumably) Tanker does nothing to clarify the situation.

Mention should be made in these pages of the 'plated' models which were used to decorate such things as cigarette boxes, ashtrays, pipeholders and penstands attractively finished in a very shiny gold or silver plating, the only colour relief being the plastic components, usually in shades differing from the production toys (see reference to plastic transplants). After starting as table ornaments a number of these are finding their way on to the Swapmeet and Toy Fair scene frequently detached from their original bases. The only thing that can really be said about them is that the plating chips rather badly and is impossible to refurbish and plastic seats do not take kindly to having cigarette ends stubbed out on them, as a result of which the seats are often missing anyway. Some of these plated models may also be found with coloured baseplates, but however attractive they might appear the plated portions are just as fragile. The only plated model issued as a Yesteryear proper remains the widely sold Sunbeam motor cycle and side-car combination, and it is the chromed finish of this (which is more robust than that used on the table furniture cars) which generates the most criticism of this beautifully detailed little model.

If it is thought that this background to the Yesteryear scene concentrates too much on the cars rather than the different forms of locomotion represented by the first issue in the series, this may indeed be true though as has been stated elsewhere, the reason for this is found in the many years which passed between the demise of the old, and the introduction of the new generation of 'commercials'. During this period the expression 'Yesteryears' simply referred to collectable vintage cars except to those specialising in the collection of traction engines, lorries and locos who had by then turned their attention to other manufacturers anyway, since in their particular fields Lesney Yesteryears had come and gone.

The illustrations in the following pages show examples of more or less all the basic Yesteryears issued from 1956 until the end of 1983.

Why 1983? Well it seemed that although the financial problems which ultimately overtook the company stemmed from some time earlier, it did not become particularly noticeable to the collecting fraternity until the first of the models released by the successor company became evident by the wording on the baseplates. This changed from Lesney Industries to Matchbox Toys Ltd. and at the same time seemed to mark the end of a fairly identifiable chapter in the collectors' world – and hopefully the beginning of another. All the models shown are pure Lesney or early Matchbox Toys releases of Lesney engineered models and all were generally available 'over the counter' somewhere (which has been the criterion for their inclusion), though not necessarily the UK.

Not included in the guide are the special editions produced exclusively for members of the official Matchbox Clubs, both at home and abroad, which were not on sale to the general public but were manufactured in limited quantities, usually on a one

model per member basis reflecting the Club's membership at the time of production. A steady increase in membership numbers has resulted in more and more people chasing the same handful of models which have acquired something of a 'cult' image, and while they are highly sought after in some quarters they are frankly disliked in others. Their omission in no way casts doubts on their authenticity as genuine Yester-year productions as were the table furniture embellishments but, like the limited runs of promotional models presented to company employees which have also been omitted, it was felt that if they could not be bought by the collecting public as the toys they were intended to be, and as they were issued, they were not eligible for this guide.

REGD U.S PAT OFF
MARCA REGISTRADA
"MATCHBOX"
Y-14
"MODELS OF YESTERYEAR"
1911 MAXWELL ROADSTER
MATCHBOX REGD T.M G.B AND ABROAD
A LESNEY PRODUCT
MADE IN ENGLAND
Y-14
MAXWELL ROADSTER
NEW MODEL
MATCH
COLLECTOR'S CATALO

Motor Cars

Y1 1911 Ford Model T

'Any colour you like as long as its black' – though one school of thought contends that Henry Ford said this in 1917 so these 1911 cars are probably more authentic by being any colour *but* black. One of the most famous cars of all time, some 15 million being produced in 19 years, the Model 'T' laid down the almost universal spares availability which was a 'Ford' by-word for years. The introduction of the £1 per Horse-power tax in 1921 (based on RAC rating) meant that towards the end 'Tin Lizzie' paid as much road tax as a small Rolls which did not do much for its continuing use in the UK. The red car was issued from 1964, fitted with attractively realistic large diameter wheels which would considerably enhance the current Y12 vans even though these are to a larger scale. The white one some 10 years later utilised the smaller wheels and thick tyres shown, which is a common feature of so many models issued in second colour schemes from 1973 onwards. The shiny smooth hood mounted on the red one gave way to a hood having a textured finish which may be found in both colours. A defect sometimes arising on the red model is that one or other of the side-lamps is missing, leaving a small neat knob on the scuttle where it should have been. The unpainted windscreen frame of the white car may show signs of corrosion.

Y1 1936 Jaguar (!) SS100

The 'Champagne Special' which outgrew and outper-
formed its original 'play-boy' image to become, after
some notable Rally successes, one of the most respected
sports cars of all. Oddly enough the practice of calling
these cars Jaguar SS100s is of relatively recent origin.
Until the mid-1960s one spoke of SS100s or of Jaguars,
the latter being the model name for the SS company's
contemporary sports saloon introduced in 1936,
although in fact all SS cars were officially termed
Jaguar from 1937 onwards and the company name had
changed to that in 1945, some 20 years earlier. This
attractive two-seater was first issued as a Yesteryear in
1977 finished in a creamy white frequently having
slight chips in the paint surface from new. The original
models in this colour had ugly, rather lumpy sidelights,
but these gave way to rounded, much neater ones quite
early on. This version was followed by the metallic blue
job in 1979. In 1981 the colour changed again to a
handsome dark green, but it is an elegant car in any
colour and it would be nice to see the black or the
possibly less common red ones appear in the range.

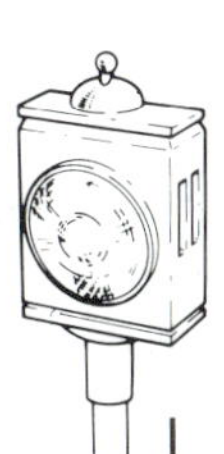

Y2 1911 Renault

Car manufacture was almost a hobby for Louis Renault before he enlisted the assistance of brothers Marcel and Fernand to help found a business producing a range of De-Dion engined two-cylinder cars, supplemented by four-cylinder models from 1902 onwards. Renaults were notable for their use of Cardan shaft drive from the very beginning, in place of the then more usual chain drive. Against this quite advanced feature is set their retention of the scuttle mounted radiator for many years after other manufacturers had abandoned it. This little two-cylinder 8 HP model is dated 1911, though small lower-powered Renaults looking remarkably like it may be seen every year taking part in the annual Brighton Run (which is restricted to cars made before 1905). The model was issued from 1963 when so many Yesteryears were painted in eye-catching, if unrealistic, metallic colours. Only produced in green although the shades may vary. The metallic finishes also tend to fade much more, giving an even greater range of shades. Early models had metal steering wheels painted green which are frequently slightly loose and wobbly, later ones were black plastic. Spare wheel carriers may be three or four-pronged, the three-pronged ones being common to several Yesteryear models, and the seat was used later on for the early white Y4 Opels.

Y2 1914 Vauxhall 'Prince Henry'

Mention the pre-First World War Prince Henry Trials and the Continental collector will think of such makes as Austro-Daimler, Benz, Mercedes and Metallurgique. To the UK enthusiast Prince Henry automatically means the Pomeroy Vauxhall with its attractively pointed radiator and abbreviated fluting of which both two and four-seat versions survive. The red model with the magnificent spoked wheels was first issued in 1970 and was one of the first 'classic' Yesteryears when Lesney quality matched anything else on the toy/model market at twice the price. The metallic blue car from 1975 and the red and black one with white-wall tyres, which appeared in 1979, lost something when they reverted to the standard small diameter wheels. The blue model was originally shown in the 1975 catalogue with bright red seats, but in the event all 'Prince Henrys' emerged on to the UK market with off-white plastic seats which rather lower the tone, though red-seated ones undoubtedly exist. The seats from the Y13 Daimler fit this car so beware any trimmed in black or maroon.

Y3 1910 Benz Limousine

It is not until the significance of the small scale of this model sinks in – 54:1 being the second smallest scale for any of the Yesteryear cars – that one realises what a very imposing vehicle the original must be, lending very real meaning to the immortal (and contemporary) definition of a sports car as 'any car you cannot *walk* through with your hat on!'. First issued in 1966 in cream with a dark green roof, then in medium green with a light yellow-green roof sometimes described as Chartreuse, much less frequently with the black roof more usually associated with the darker metallic green which was the final body colour catalogued from 1970. The second colour, although not a particularly scarce model, seems a bit thin on the ground at times, (the one pictured here was bought in Austria in 1967) though much less so than the third which seems to have been an interim 'between batches' production that can be difficult to find and yet, until quite recently, not expensive to acquire. The Chartreuse-roofed version may have a red or dark green radiator grille. Early issues of the model had the headlights centred slightly above the front wings, later ones slightly below. Handle this one with care, the rear seat drops out very easily.

Y3 1934 Riley MPH

A very pretty little sports car from the mid-1930s produced by a motor manufacturer 'As Old as the Industry – As Modern as the Hour' whose products, even the more sedate ones, always had an air of the sports car about them and whose sports cars generated enormous enthusiasm among the Riley fraternity. The MPH, of which only a limited number was built before the company was absorbed into the Nuffield organisation, was no exception. This model was introduced into the Yesteryear range in 1974 in an engaging if highly improbable metallic red, which varied considerably from light red to quite a pronounced purple. This version is particularly prone to fading in strong sunlight. Later on, in about 1979, the colour changed to a medium blue, although retaining the rather cheap looking cream coloured plastic seats, with the addition of racing numbers 6, 3 or 9. This model last appeared in the 1981/1982 catalogue.

36

Y4 1909 Opel

Old established cycle makers before entering the motor industry via connections with Lutzmann and Darracq, Opels established a reputation for producing sturdy, reliable motor cars during the early days of this century. They remained very much a family firm until taken over by General Motors in 1929. This is a nicely proportioned little model of the Opel 4/8, known as the 'Doctors' Coupe' from the medical profession's predilection for open two-seaters which, from the number of cars to bear this description over the years, lasted well into the 1930s. The white car was issued from 1967 and like so many 'first colour' cars had large wheels. These, if not individual to the car, were at least not out of proportion or style as were the small diameter, thick tyred wheels fitted as standard to so many 'second colour' cars like the orange one shown here. The latter was available from about 1973. Early white models had the hood attached to body pegs at all four positions, later white, and all the orange versions used pegs on the plastic seat for the side attachments while retaining the body pegs for the rear ones. Tan coloured hoods may be smooth surfaced or textured, black ones for the orange model had a textured finish.

Y4 1930 Duesenberg Model J

Motoring writers tend to run out of superlatives when faced with the Duesenberg Model J and the supercharged SJ. Suffice it to say that they are usually considered to be the ultimate in American luxury cars, frequently bodied by the leading coachbuilders of the period. This is a handsome, rather elegant model which is unfortunate because it lacks the essential 'beefiness' of this really very large car, particularly if it is stood beside anything else ostensibly to the same scale of 43:1. One theory suggests that the model is of the long-chassis car actually scaled at 47:1. This is the base model for the famous White-name-your-own-price-Duesenberg, the rarest of Yesteryears for which release figures ranging from the modest to the minimal are quoted. (Genuine examples of which may be identified by the triangular cut-outs in the top panel). To the average buyer it emerged in a rich metallic red in 1976 to be followed in two-tone green for the 1979/80 presentation, the rear body panel being in either of the two greens, the later more common version utilising the green of the bonnet top and baseplate rather than that of the body sides. This colour scheme gave way to an equally attractive two-tone brown for 1983. The chromed wheels may be multi-spoked or dished and the black or green plastic parts of the two earlier models may sometimes be found interchanged.

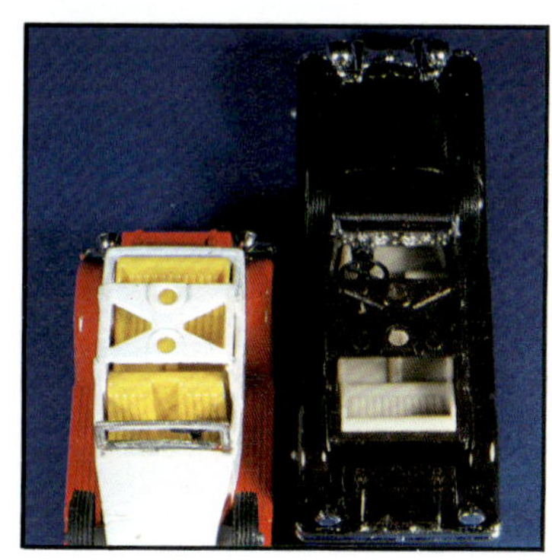

Y5 1929 Bentley Le Mans

Model manufacturers contemplating the addition of a racing Bentley to their ranges have always been obsessed with the supercharged version of the $4^1/_2$ litre cars (which in fact never won a major race) and Lesney were no exception. The 1929 Le Mans team cars were not supercharged and yet this little model of a short-chassis $4^1/_2$ clearly sports a 'blower' between its dumbirons. This is one of the original cars in the range, introduced in 1958, and is an attractive albeit quite tiny model by later Yesteryear standards. At a scale of 55:1 its only shelf companion is the original issue of the Rolls-Royce 'Silver Ghost'. Initially it was fitted with the solid wheels on clenched axles, though later ones had the axles riveted which improved the appearance quite noticeably. Early wheels also seem to be unplated, and dull down rather badly. The radiator shell may be painted either silver or gold, leaving the radiator grille green. The seats and rear tonneau cover may also be green in place of the red and grey of the model shown.

Y5 1929 4^{1}/$_{2}$ lt. (S) Bentley

A larger scale model of a long-chassis 4^{1}/$_{2}$, this time identifiable as one of the Birkin Blower team cars. Though at 52:1, still one of the smaller Yesteryears, the increase in scale permits a more satisfying model with a greater scope for improved detail including headlights, finely spoked wheels and mounting steps. This larger version first came out in 1962 and was painted overall, including the radiator shell though not the grille, in a green which always had a slightly metallic look about it. This probably varied with the paint thickness, early ones having a very pronounced sheen indeed. The original shade is usually described as 'apple green', but models in anything like this colour would appear to be extremely elusive. A suspicion that this appellation is applied to equally rare, slightly lighter-hued models finished in a sort of 'metallic mildew', reminiscent of the patina on well weathered copper, should not be discounted. At different times during the production run, the green lost its metallic look to become much richer in colour. The tonneau and seats changed from green to bright red later a duller red and the radiator became a separate casting with a frequently rather dull silver finish. Racing numbers on the silver radiator cars may be 6, 3 or 5 in that order.

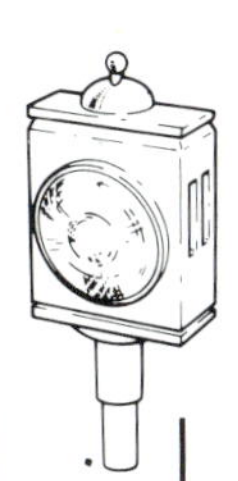

Y5 1907 Peugeot

Manufacturing ironmongers from Napoleonic times and cycle makers from 1885 before extending their activities to the production of motor cars, Peugeot have a claim to being the oldest car company in the world. (Vauxhalls, with their roots in the iron foundry business from at least a century earlier, did not enter this field until 1903). This model of the chain-driven 12/16 HP car was issued in 1969 in yellow and black, to be followed by the gold one with a dull or matt black baseplate some four or so years later. The shades of gold employed on the latter vary quite considerably, some even having a faint but quite noticeable pink or orange cast, and since the upper and lower portions of the body are finished separately two quite different shades can appear on the same model. The black topped version of this one is sometimes described as the US issue. The windows on both colours may be amber tinted or plain, while the yellow car has early type wheels both these and the later type shown here may be found on the gold one, which may also sometimes be found with green or red seats in place of the standard black.

46

Y6 1923 Bugatti Type 35

Of all the Bugatti racing car models on the market, and the outstanding 1990 cc Type 35 is surely the one most frequently encountered, the little Yesteryear must be one of the simplest and neatest. This one was introduced in 1961 in a quite realistic Bugatti blue. A scale of 48:1 (actually nearer 47:1) makes it a fairly large model when compared with the cars then existing in the range, but at the same time it could not really afford to be much smaller than it is. A particular point of interest is the reproduction of Bugatti's cast alloy wheels, the originals of which had the spokes slightly pitched to force cooling air on to the integral brake drums. The blue car was followed after about five years by the red one which, as well as being sold in the toyshops, was given away by garages selling a famous brand of petrol on presentation of a full set of the picture cards issued with each gallon. Treat this model with care, the paint on the sharper edges of the bodywork, tail and bonnet louvres is not very resistant to handling and comes off fairly easily. The gold finish on the radiator and the transfers are also vulnerable.

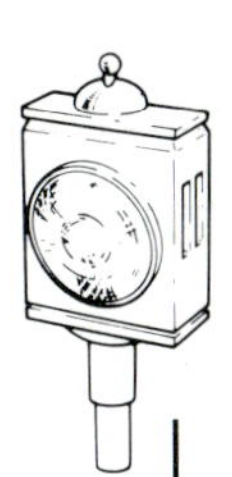

Y6 1913 Cadillac

The Cadillac company, founded in 1902, grew from an engineering works producing some of the most highly regarded automobile components of the period before turning over to the manufacture of complete cars. Cadillacs were awarded the Dewar Trophy for achievement in automotive engineering both in 1908 for an outstanding degree of interchangeability, and in 1913, for the introduction of the electric starting fitted to their cars as standard from 1912. This is a nicely proportioned, rather attractive little model, though the metallic yellow colouring is a bit fierce. This one was produced from 1967. The metallic green followed it some six or seven years later, as indicated by the type of wheels fitted. The maroon hood on the yellow version may be of the early smooth or the later textured type. Paint shades and the colour of plastic items such as seats and grilles can vary a lot on this model. A scale of 48:1 makes this a good stable-mate for some of the other contemporary American cars in the range – Y8 Stutz, Y9 Simplex and Y12 Thomas.

Y7 1913 Mercer Raceabout

The raceabout style of body fitted to this little Mercer Type 35J always had a certain amount of appeal, even though it would frighten the life out of the people who frame the Construction and Use regulations for the 1980s. Weather protection (when fitted) was also a bit spartan, consisting of a single circular glass windscreen not much larger than the steering wheel above which it was mounted by means of a bracket fitted to the column. Suffice it to say that the Mercers acquired a racing reputation which became legendary, despite a habit of breaking chassis frames. This model, only about the sixth or seventh car to be issued in the Yesteryear range, came out in 1961 in a colour best described as metallic violet, in fact ranging from almost mid-violet to little more than 'tinted silver'. A tendency to fade badly does not improve the colour definition. A rather frail little model with increasing reinforcement added to the casting as production continued. The yellow car was available from about 1966 in a shade which can only be described as 'hearty' – somehow the model in this colour loses the fragile look of the earlier ones even though it is a little more authentic.

Y7 1912 Rolls-Royce

Only the collectors who were buying their Yesteryears as they were issued in the '50s and '60s will fully appreciate the irresistible appeal of the Rolls landaulette as it first appeared in 1968. Only the second of the larger scale, formal closed cars (the Y3 Benz preceded it by a couple of years) it joined the Yesteryear range at a time when open, occasionally rather spartan, two and four-seaters were more in evidence than anything else. These were also largely 'one-colour' cars, only the plastic components and brightwork providing any colour relief, so that this little beauty in its attractive, if unrealistic, silver and bright red was really quite something. The gold version came along a few years later and is equally impressive despite the later type wheels. The roofs on these models were initially smooth surfaced, but the later ones were ribbed at the rear end and the red paint sometimes acquired a slightly metallic finish. Some silver versions had metallic grey roofs during the changeover from smooth to ribbed castings, and tend to be expensive if these are of the latter type. Spare wheel carriers may also vary, earlier ones being in outline rather than the full dish worn by the later ones. The yellow and black car with red wheels was the last issue of this model from about 1979/1980, being dropped from the catalogue for 1983.

Y8 1926 'Bullnose' Morris Cowley

This tiny, rather dainty, little model was one of the original cars in the Yesteryear range, produced from 1958 onwards. Compared with the larger scale 'exotica' introduced later – the Rolls, Hispanos and Mercs – it looks a very 'bread and butter' little motor car indeed which of course it was, although it made its own significant contribution to motoring history. This is one of the cars which pre-dates Lesney's later policy of producing each model in several colour schemes, and the one used here is very typical for a 1920s Morris. Not many variations with this model. The paint shades vary a little and the axles changed from the clenched to the riveted type during the production run. Some wheels also dull down more than others. These Morrises have been seen with the gold paint missing from the radiator, though whether this results from excessive handling or a missed stage during manufacture is a matter for conjecture.

Y8 1914 Stutz Type 4E

An attractive model of a handsome car bearing a name famous for both its quality and the makes' sporting associations. This two-seat roadster was the last of the batch of pre-WW1 American cars which Lesney issued to the same scale in the later 1960s, first appearing in 1969 in the metallic red shown here. Although a relatively small model consisting of few basic parts the car wears an opulent, well-fed look, probably as a result of its 'wide-body' proportions. The small diameter wheels on the blue one show it to be a later issue of the model, available from about 1973. The colour shades can vary not only between model and model, but also between body and baseplate. Early hoods had a smooth finish which gave way to a textured finish later. These later hoods also incorporated an additional pair of clips at mid-position enabling them to fit other models, the Crossley lorry being one such. The weak point is the wedges at the rear edge of the hood which break off very easily.

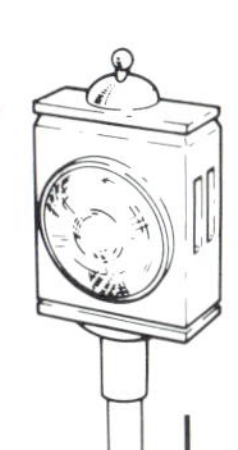

Y8 1945 MG TC

'Classic Sports Car in the Traditional Mould' – or upholstered roller skate for the rapid transport of masochistic contortionists – take your choice, but the little MGs were quite fun and the passage of time coupled with a tinge of nostalgia softens the memories of some of their more irritating characteristics. The green model first appeared in 1978 and may have red or tan coloured seats. The racing numbers were progressively 3, 6 or 9. For 1981 the colour was changed to red, with black seats. Some red ones were released in 1982 with the hoods in a plastic rather more red than the standard colour. These are usually described as 'red hood' MGs though the colour is not as intense as the description would imply. The green and red models are in more or less the right colours for the TC, but the blue one, issued in 1983, is less authentic, MG factory blue being several shades lighter in colour than that used for this model which may be found with tan or black seats and standard or 'red' hoods. A feature of these cars, not possible with the chromed plastic radiators, is that the radiator bars were frequently painted with non-shiny, bright, almost poster colour paints and white cars with red bars, dark green cars with light apple-green bars and pale blue cars with medium blue bars were the norm.

Y9 1912 Simplex Model 50

Not to be confused with the Mercedes-Simplex or the American Simplex this make resulted from the desire of the sole US importers of Fiat, Renault, Panhard and Mercedes cars to produce the best automobile of comparable quality that could be built in America. The Yesteryear Simplex seems to have been around for ever since a light green one first appeared in 1968. Later the colour darkened, though the paint used may still be seen to vary if models from different batches are stood side by side. Initially the hood was secured to metal pegs on the body, but quite early on during the life of the darker issue the pegs were transferred to the plastic seats. The hood acquired a textured finish at about the same time. The gold and red version dates from about 1970 and seems to be less common than the others. The red car with the black hood was produced from 1973 until 1979 when it was superseded by the red and black one with the rather garish yellow top. This last appeared in the 1981/82 catalogue. As in so many cases the style of wheels fitted helps to differentiate between the earlier and later models. Check this one carefully, the front seat drops out easily and the moulded handrail behind it is fragile. Replacement hoods are also difficult to come by.

Y10 1908 Mercedes GP

The biggest problem with this little model of one of the early giant-engined (12.8 litre) racing cars is that it is too small to be fully appreciated. Dimensionally suitable to comprise the contents of a mildly up-market Christmas cracker it suffers from the fact that it was one of the small scale original cars in the range, though it lacks the dignity of the Bentley or the daintiness of the Morris. At a scale of 54:1 its sole shelf-mate is the Y3 Benz, and when placed beside this it only emphasises the majestic proportions of that very imposing carriage. That said, it's a nice little car that deserves a better Press than it usually gets. First issued in 1958 this model has very few variations though the precise shades of white paint may vary slightly and the gold painted items may sometimes be painted silver or left white. Clenched axles on the early ones gave way to riveted axles, and the wheels range from the brightly plated to the sort which dull down rather badly. The axles and steering column are very prone to rust on this model.

Y10 1928 Mercedes-Benz 36/220 S-type

When shown at the London Motor Show in 1927 – the first time that Mercedes had shown anything there since before the First World War – the S-type attracted a lot of attention with its low-slung chassis and Porsche-developed, Rootes-type supercharger. It went on to figure conspicuously on the motor-sport scene, despite its lack of braking ability, before the SS and SSK models came along. This quite smart Yesteryear came out in 1963 to a scale of 52:1, which is fairly small, but it goes nicely with the larger of the two contemporary Bentleys. The white body with red and fawn interior is quite attractive, though the radiator casting is frequently a bit porous. The only significant variation on this car is that early ones had two spare wheels, later ones had only one. Handle this model carefully, the front seat drops out very easily and, as is the case with so many Yesteryear plastic components, an unfaded replacement can be difficult to locate.

66

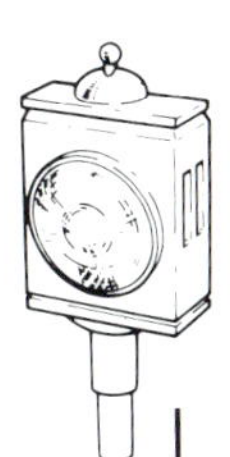

Y10 1906 Rolls-Royce 'Silver Ghost'

A nice standard Ghost which looks like becoming a contender for the longest produced car in the series. It is, in effect, an enlarged though not quite identical copy of the original Y15 Ghost – the fourth car in the range introduced in 1960. This one first appeared in 1969 in a colour scheme which almost defies description, a sort of metallic lime-green and gunmetal. Around 1973 the colour changed to white, with a baseplate ranging from faintly metallic light red, almost pink, to a near scarlet metallic finish. The styles of wheel fitted follow the usual pattern. The all-silver version emerged in 1979 and has always been pictured with red or maroon seats and white-wall tyres, though the yellow-seated variant shown here is supposed to be equally common and certainly turned up in some shops at the time, but it is not particularly conspicuous on the Toy Fair scene now. This model suffered a lot from windscreen distortion during manufacture, the vertical section being tilted forward or back, and while this can be straightened by hand it is an exercise not to be undertaken lightly – it breaks very easily.

Y11 1912 Packard Landaulette

From 1903, when the Ohio Automobile concern became the Packard Motor Company, the make always enjoyed a reputation for being a good sound motor car in the luxury bracket, this modestly proportioned landaulette exemplifying the smaller 'town carriage' of its period. The 4 cylinder 25 HP Model 18 from which this Yesteryear was probably scaled has been the subject of several offerings from die-cast and, more particularly, plastic kit manufacturers. The Lesney version appeared on the scene in 1964 though the small size, and simplicity of the semi-closed body casting, seems to be more consistent with the pre-1960 releases than with the bulkier, riveted assemblies which characterised the other closed cars issued in the mid 1960s. It was turned out only in the one colour scheme though the shades of red may vary. The later ones appear a bit brighter. The steering wheel was usually metal, but some later issue plastic ones may be found, and the four point spare wheel carrier was followed by a three point one. Clean this model with care, the crested transfers on the doors can be disconcertingly fragile.

Y11 1938 Lagonda Drophead Coupe

There has always been a slightly aristocratic air about the Lagondas of the late 1930s with their flowing lines and helmet-type spare wheel covers (even if one of them was a dummy one concealing tools and wheel jack). That they were very fast and very luxurious merely adds to the magnetism of these lovely W.O. Bentley-engineered cars. This LG45 was first produced in 1972 in a handsome rather than pretty metallic gold, with a very dark purple baseplate. Later baseplates were more red in colour, and a few light red ones also exist, this version sometimes being described as the 'strawberry' Lagonda which is very rare indeed. The metallic orange car with the bronze baseplate dates from a year or so later, and the body colour ranges from a metallic salmon pink to a very rich metallic red, the 'gingery' one depicted being somewhere in mid-range and probably the most common. For 1979 the colour changed yet again to beige and black, with the previously black seats and boot in dark red and utilising a chrome radiator and screen in place of the anachronistic brass items sported by the earlier versions. In the event this model, although a little more realistic, looks somewhat pedestrian beside the other two.

Y12 1909 Thomas 'Flyabout'

Model 'K' 6-70

One of the famous names lost when the United States Motors combine crashed in 1912, the Thomas company is better remembered for the Thomas Flyer which as the second of three finishers, and after the penalties were worked out, was declared the winner of the New York – Paris Race in 169 days in 1908. The Model 'K' 6-70 was claimed to be the fastest luxury car in series production, and to have the most comprehensive equipment fit. The Yesteryear model is not a bad one either, issued from 1967 in varying shades of metallic blue and from about 1973 in even more shades of metallic red or magenta – sometimes described as 'from Beaujolais to Vin Rosé', the usual first reaction to the latter being 'ouch'. The red seats of the blue model may be found in yellow, though not very often as this is one of the notorious 'rarities'. The hood acquired a textured finish and started picking up on seat instead of body pegs during the blue cars' production run. Wheels and spare tyre carriers also changed in the usual way, the later three-lug type carrier being widely used on a number of Yesteryear models.

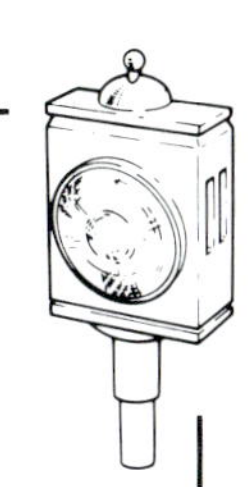

YI3 I9II Daimler Type AI2

Like the Prince Henry Vauxhall described elsewhere the model of the smaller open Daimler is one of those Yesteryears which could, indeed it did, match anything else on the market at a much higher price. This one really is quite a miniature masterpiece with its beautifully reproduced large diameter spoked wheels and typically ribbed Daimler radiator. True, that radiator should probably be cast aluminium alloy rather than brass, but in view of the overall quality of the model few people would argue. First produced in 1966 it retained a yellow and black finish for the whole of its production life, and must have been about the last of the Yesteryear cars issued in only the one colour scheme. The shades of yellow may vary quite considerably, the later ones being darker in colour. They also had the spare wheel box on the running board cut away to become open sided. Early seats were black, later ones were dark red though the radiator grilles frequently remained black. The radiator grille is the great weakness of this model – it almost always drops out, and the colour does not lend itself to easy retrieval.

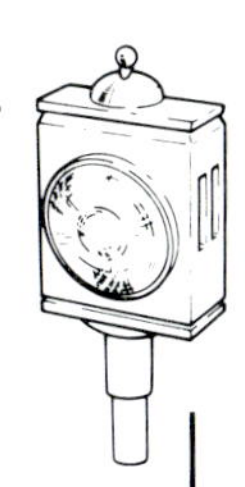

Y14 1911 Maxwell Model GA Roadster

An early Maxwell advertising slogan proclaimed 'Perfectly Simple and Simply Perfect'. A little sweeping perhaps, but a later slogan was 'The Maxwell Is A Good Car' which might more readily apply to this little model issued from 1965. Still on the small side, although it wasn't a very large car anyway but, ignoring some of the larger scaled 'small' cars such as the Renault and Bugatti, it does fall between the early 'tinies' and the later 'hefties' which have appeared in the Yesteryear range. Produced to a scale of 49:1 – so near and yet so far from the 48:1 pre- First World War Americana beside which it looks insignificant, though the simple, quite pleasant colour scheme may partly account for that. Only issued in the one colour though most photographs make it look a bit blue. Most variations seem to be minor casting ones though gold or copper petrol tanks, copper, silver or gold fire extinguishers and later textured hoods, may be found which are interchangeable with the Y8 Stutz. Radiator grilles may be black or red and fall out fairly easily. A version with unplated brightwork is also sometimes rumoured, though the ease with which this would tarnish renders the occasional description 'silver' highly optimistic.

Y14 1931 Stutz 'Bearcat'

Made by a company whose pre-First World War Bearcats gave the Mercer Raceabouts a run for their money, and who put the wind up Bentleys in the 1928 Le Mans when a type BB finished a close second, after completing the race with a damaged gearbox. The Type DV32 bearing the revived Bearcat name was the last, and some would contend the most desirable, of the Stutz company's cars. This model was first issued in 1974 in assorted shades of metallic green, in most cases the baseplate being darker than the body though between the lighter shades of the darker colour and the darker shades of the lighter one, some cars are almost mono-tone. Early models had three vertical supports to the luggage grid, later changed to four. Some early ones were also marked 1973 underneath though this was later altered to 1974. After about five years the colour was changed to the red and cream shown. Initially these were smooth bodied and the paint joint was frequently oversprayed and rather messy. A ridge was added to the body profile to provide better separation for the colours though for some time this didn't seem to improve things very much. The white and green car dates from 1981. The radiator grille on this is usually red, though black ones may also be found.

Y15 1907 Rolls-Royce Silver Ghost

Perhaps the most extraordinary thing about this little car is how much it exemplified the dearth of decently cheap mass-produced models of Veteran cars on sale in the 1950s, as opposed to plastic kit ones which were by then becoming popular and plentiful. Viewed from some twenty-plus years after its introduction when it can now be compared with the larger, sometimes exotically coloured, frequently quite complex Yesteryears of more recent times, it is a very simple little model indeed and if placed beside one of the bulkier productions from the 1970s tends to look like a child's pedal car. First introduced and widely welcomed in 1960 this was the fourth Yesteryear car following, and of a size consistent with, the earlier Bentley, Morris and Mercedes GP. It was always finished in a light metallic green though like all the metallic paints the colours will vary. The seats and tyres were mostly black, though early models had grey tyres and some late ones have been found with green seats. Although this is such a simple little job it seems to have been credited with more casting, plating, wheel and tyre variations than all of the others. A curious feature of this model is that it bears a number plate, making it identifiable, while the larger 'Ghost', produced some nine years later, is not similarly equipped and remains anonymous

Y15 1930 Packard Victoria

The language of motoring is rich in the vocabulary of the old horse-drawn carriage builders. 'Berlin' and 'Berlinetta' have been familiar Continental forms of *carrosserie* for years, a number of electrically powered vehicles in the early years of the century were termed 'Broughams', the 300 year old 'Cabriolet' of Parisian origin has been revived in recent times for what were once described as 'Drophead Coupes', and the expression 'Landaulette' is not unknown to Yesteryear collectors. The Dietrich-designed 'Victoria' coachwork on this Packard is a far cry from the 'low four-wheeled two-seater carriage with a raised seat for the driver and a calash top' but it is, none the less, a quietly handsome beast. Issued originally in 1969 in the bronze colour which, although vaguely metallic in finish, is subdued enough for it not to look like a refugee from a fairground. The metallic yellow car, a little brighter, shared the brown baseplate of the earlier one, but off-set this with a hood and boot – sorry, top and trunk – in black in place of the dark red. This colour scheme dates from 1973. The third version in 'straight' black and red was issued in 1979 when colors were rather more realistic though the white hood is, to anybody who has lived with a white-hooded motor car or avoided doing so, little short of a disaster.

Y16 1904 (!) Spyker

A Dutch car made in Trompenberg by a company the excellence of whose two and four-cylinder offerings was widely admired and which so impressed the Bradford Motor Company in 1903 that they contracted to take the entire Spyker production for the subsequent three years. The circular radiator was a characteristic of Spyker cars among others, and was retained until the make ceased production in 1925, although by then it had acquired a rather more rounded form. This model bears a number plate identifying it as the (VCC-dated) 1905 4 cylinder 12/18 HP vehicle which became so well known to a world-wide cinema-going public in 1953, first appearing as a Yesteryear in 1961 in a pale creamy colour. About the fifth, at most the seventh car in the range it retains the simplicity of the previous releases. As time went by, the colour progressively darkened to a rich yellow, and the late cars lost the gold paint round the radiator shell and headlamp which makes them look a little unfinished. This is a sturdy little model of a quite attractive motor car and until fairly recently seemed to be about the only representative of this make on the model scene.

Y16 1928 Mercedes-Benz SS Coupe

Among the Yesteryear quality cars Mercedes have featured rather more prominently than any other make and few collectors, particularly those representing the international markets, would argue with this choice when the resulting products are such pleasing models. Nobody buying the original silver and red issue of the SS Coupe when it first appeared in 1972 could have guessed that some ten or a dozen years later the model would enjoy such a revival of interest as that seen during the last few years. That version was followed by one in metallic green, the shades of which vary so much that 'light' and 'dark' ones are recognised – discounting an exceptional and rare batch released with Stutz-green baseplates literally 'two-tone' cars are not uncommon. During the production run of this issue the original separately cast exhaust system was incorporated into the baseplate casting, also some cars were released with the standard black plastic components in dark green. These latter are infrequently encountered and tend to be in a higher price bracket. For 1979 the body and baseplate changed to a rather severe white which, with its black accessories and by now silver radiator casting makes for quite a striking model. The version in blue and grey appeared in 1981, by which time the castings were becoming noticeably coarser. Although the standard colouring by the end of 1983 remained blue and grey, the grey areas may be found painted pale blue, ostensibly for the European market where they were certainly quite plentiful in Germany and Switzerland, and later a pale creamy brown.

Y17 1938 Hispano-Suiza

Designed by a Swiss engineer, financed by Spanish businessmen and ultimately built in France bearing an emblem from Alsace. Such is the international background of the Hispano-Suiza which rivalled in excellence the Rolls-Royce itself. Like Rolls they raced with moderate success before the First World War, but in post-war years concentrated on building motor cars of the highest quality. Also like Rolls, they extended their activities into the aero-engine field during that war and it is from their aeronautical associations that they acquired the 'Cicogne Volante' emblem, several versions of which had identified the component units of the renowned French 'Stork' fighter squadron, flying Hispano-engined SPAD aircraft. This model was first illustrated in the 1973 catalogue in silver and black, disappeared from the 1974 catalogue and arrived eventually in 1975 in a pleasing, if unlikely, metallic red and black. Equally attractive was the version which appeared about four years later in metallic and light blue. This scheme lost something of its ethereal look in 1981 when the wings were changed to black, which was the colour combination still catalogued in 1983.

Y18 1937 Cord 812

This car was developed as a supercharged version of the 810, the advanced styling of which was originally planned by Auburn engineer Gordon Buehrig for a smaller, less expensive Duesenberg. Fifteen years later in 1952 the design was chosen by the American Museum of Modern Art as an outstanding example of modern coachwork. For the enthusiast who appreciates the somewhat 'futuristic' approach of so many 1930s products – the Chrysler 'Airflow' was another one – the model is very easy on the eye too, though it looks a bit odd when stood beside some of the 'early perpendicular' Yesteryears. It was first issued in 1979 in bright red, though the white hood grates a bit and shows up finger-marks rather badly. In 1983 the colour changed to a subdued maroon while the white plastic items were retained. The wheels on the red model are always illustrated in the catalogue as the plated dished type, but finely spoked wheels and unplated (red) dished ones have also been found on this version.

Y19 1933 Auburn 851 Speedster

Founded in 1900 at Auburn, Indiana, the Auburn company had by the 1930s earned a reputation for building good fast cars at a reasonable price though their road-holding has been described as less suited to European roads. Viewed from the 1980s they may be better remembered for their connections with the people whose names feature frequently in American motoring history, albeit when viewed from an English viewpoint, in which Erret Cord, Gordon Buehrig, the Duesenberg brothers and Ab Jenkins keep cropping up. The 851 'Speedster' is perhaps the best car to represent this company on a collector's shelf and this model first appeared in a sort of coffee and cream colour scheme in the 1980/81 catalogue. It's a nice 'chunky' sort of model though its rather a pity that one or two of the associated makes are not to the same scale. The white car, which would have been better without the black wings, appeared in 1983. The wheels shown on the brown and cream model when first catalogued were of the chrome-plated dished type but, though these can be found, most seem to be unplated and red which rather clashes with the paintwork.

Y20 1938 Mercedes-Benz 540K

A magnificently appointed, large and comfortable touring car from a famous maker or a flamboyant, overbodied *'prunkwagen'* with a performance handicapped by its sheer weight, the 540K has attracted both praise and criticism. An improvement on the Type 500, it had in its favour a top speed in excess of 100 mph with the supercharger engaged, a quite advanced all-round independent suspension, and was fitted with some very handsome coachwork. This model, based on the Sindelfingen factory's long-tailed roadster, also received some criticism when it was first issued because of an alleged inaccuracy of line. Whether this is the case or not it is certainly very impressive. Produced in a striking silver, black and red colour scheme it first appeared in 1981. No significant variations on this model, though in the 1981/82 catalogue the seats were shown coffee coloured.

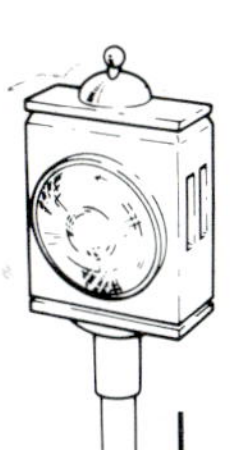

Y21 1930 Ford Model A 'Woody Wagon'

An odd little estate-car, having all the excitement of a plate of cold suet which, when it first appeared in the 1981/82 catalogue, aroused in many quarters a feeling of – why *that?* At the same time, had it been announced as a limited edition for the US market, at which it was presumably aimed, it is a safe bet that those same critics would have been scrambling over each other to obtain one. A sturdy little model which doesn't do much for the UK enthusiast it appeared in the summer of 1981 in yellow and brown, with a quite ingenious plastic utility body. The later version introduced as the 'A & J Box' van (whoever they are) came in several forms. This was initially a conversion of the original 'Woody Wagon' and on early ones the yellow paint is still evident. This 'gives the bonnet a nice glow but flakes off round the rivets'. Also in evidence is the chrome windscreen, but this disappeared from later batches. Later ones had a darker metallic paint or less often a non-metallic brown finish on the bonnet. This model is one likely to bear either the 'Lesney' or the 'Matchbox Toys Ltd' marking.

Y24 1927 Bugatti Type 44

Some car manufacturers seem never to have produced an ugly, or even plain, motor car during the whole of their production lives. Many enthusiasts consider Bugatti to have been one of them, although their styling really tended to range from the beautiful to the positively quaint. Even the racing 'Tanks' of 1923, which may have looked like high-speed woodlice, still wore an air of brutal elegance when viewed from some elevations. The coachwork on this Type 44 is so typically Bugatti, strongly influenced by Le Patron's liking for the clean lines and graceful curves of the Broughams of the last century. This styling, and others very much like it, graced several Bugatti types including one Royale and examples of it are dotted around the Motor Museums of Europe. This model was the only new car released in 1983 among several existing ones appearing in new colour schemes, and was the first Yesteryear car with glazed windows. The plated catches on the luggage boot are also a nice touch.

Motor Cycle

Y8 1914 Sunbeam Motor-Cycle

'Milford Side-Car Combination. Rarely encountered on the road these days, it is not all that many years since motorcycle and side-car combinations were a surprisingly popular form of transport. They acquired something of a reputation as the safest things on the road at one time, though whether this resulted from their layout or the fact that they were largely 'enthusiast' vehicles is open to question. Before the war they held their own with other traffic on the narrow roads of the period but, as was the case with many pre-war cars, the generation of fast family saloons which emerged in the 1950s was really too much for them and they faded out leaving a recollection of being 'too slow to follow, too wide to pass'. This exquisite little model of an early combination was produced from 1962 onwards. It does not appear to have been a very popular production, most people dislike the chrome finish relieved only by the black and green of the saddle and seat; the latter may also be found in black. Motor cyclists have commented on the absence of hand controls and footrests. It must also have been a rather fragile toy for children. Very much a 'one-off' in the Yesteryear range, but it really is beautifully detailed even though it requires a good magnifying glass to appreciate it fully.

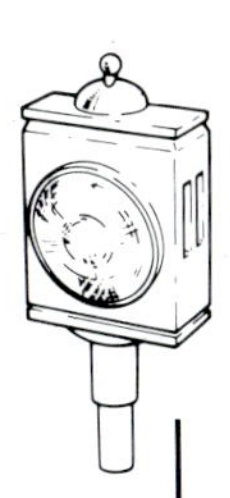

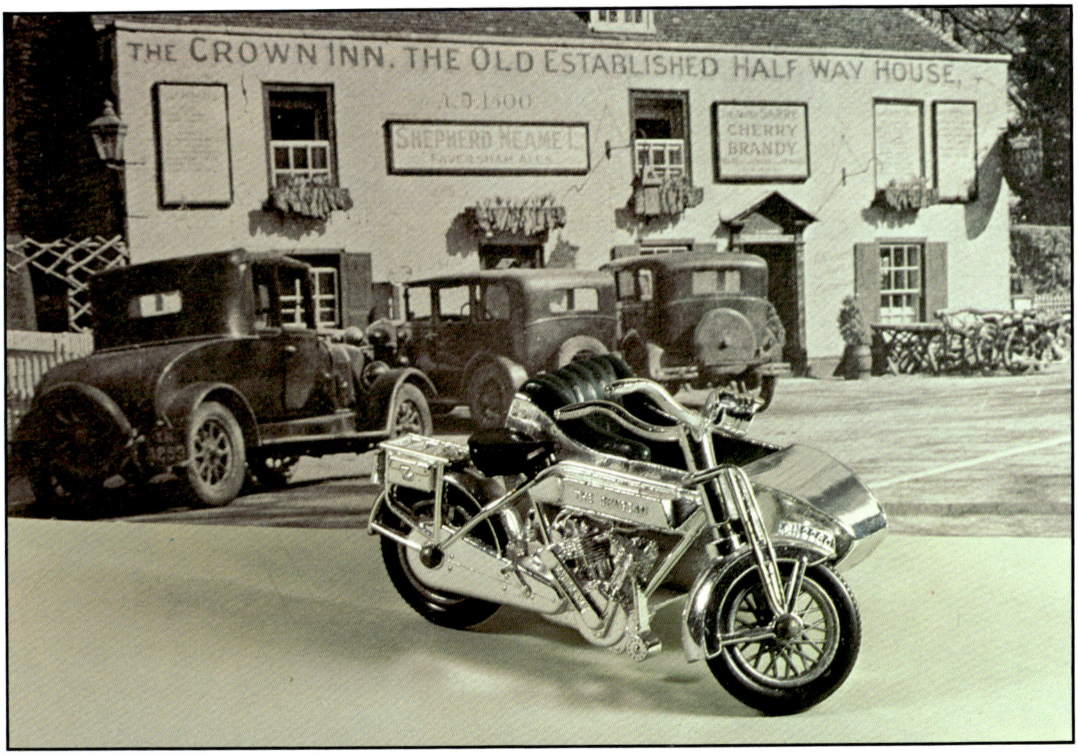
THE CROWN INN. THE OLD ESTABLISHED HALF WAY HOUSE.
A.D.1500
SHEPHERD NEAME
FAVERSHAM ALES
CHERRY
BRANDY

# Passenger Vehicles

Y2 'B' Type Bus

One of the more primitive of the Yesteryears this little bus probably owes its appeal more to nostalgia than quality, since the latter is strongly reminiscent of the cheap and cheerful 'stocking-fillers' of pre-War days. Viewed with a less critical eye, or from a greater distance, it seems to have the right look about it for the period, both in proportion and general layout, presumably resulting from the existence of an original of the type in the London Transport Museum. A scale of 100:1 makes it an ideal shelf companion for the three 1920s commercial lorries or the London General Omnibus Company's horse-drawn bus which it succeeded in 1910. This model first appeared in 1956 finished in the red always associated with London buses, bearing a driver in black, or later, a driver of several shades of blue. Not many variations with this model though early ones had four small vent windows above the main windows each side, while the later releases had these divided to form eight. The early grey wheels were later finished black.

Y3 1907 London 'E' Class Tramcar

Although this model bears the date 1907, viewed from 1956 when it was first issued, it seems an unlikely candidate for a series called Models of Yesteryear. This is because the last tram to run in London, looking remarkably like this one, had not been withdrawn until only four years earlier in 1952. From the mid 1930s onwards however, they had been progressively replaced throughout the London Transport network with trolley-buses, which themselves ceased running in 1963. Suffice it to say that the trams disappeared from the London scene leaving behind recollections of a lot of clanking and grinding noises, an unmistakeable bell tone and an equally unforgetable carbonny smell of hot electrics. This model, not one of the most sophisticated in the range, is of the type which utilised overhead cables and a long spring-hinged arm rising from the top of the tram which in this instance is in the stowed position (others were powered from underground cables). Always produced in red and with posters which varied slightly in printing style, though not content, the differences are confined to open or blocked doorways and stairs, metal wheels which were replaced with plastic ones and white roof-topping which superseded the original cream. Headlights and control panels may be gold, silver or mixed and the fenders may be grey or red.

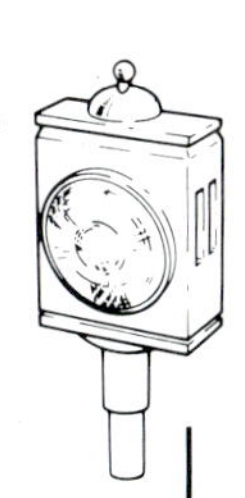

BEST SUNDAY PAPER
NEWS OF THE WORLD
WORLD'S RECORD SALE
CITY
BUY LESNEY TOYS
LONDON TRANSPORT

Y12 1899 London Horse-Drawn Bus

Like the Shand Mason Fire Engine this is another one for the horse-age enthusiast, complete with labouring team and a rather depressed looking driver. As with the Y2 model of the 'B' Type bus which replaced it, it is singularly short of conductor and passengers. To its credit it is a very dainty little affair with nicely proportioned coachwork and large, fairly delicate wheels. Modelled to the same scale of 100:1 it provides an excellent shelf companion for its motorised successor, though of course it had disappeared from the streets of London by the time the other items in the range issued to this scale came into use. During the production run of the model the horses appeared in several shades of brown, and the upper deck seats varied in hue as did the driver's mackintosh. The decals remained the same though were printed with varying intensity. The only major difference was the attachment of the horse-pole, one rivet giving way to two for the later issues.

LIPTON'S TEA
LONDON GENERAL OMNIBUS COMPANY LIMITED
VICTORIA & KING'S-CROSS

LIPTON'S TEA
LONDON GENERAL OMNIBUS COMPANY LIMITED
VICTORIA & KING'S-CROSS

# Y23 1922 AEC 'S' Type Omnibus.

A later pattern of bus than the original diminutive Y2 version, but it still utilises the outside staircase which persisted until the 1930s, although by that time the upper deck had acquired a roof. This model was keenly anticipated when it first appeared in the 1982/83 catalogue but generated a lot of disappointed correspondence when it reached the shops around mid-1983, mainly about the absence of driver and steering wheel, though no Yesteryear had been issued with the former for nearly 20 years. Modelled to a scale of 72:1, so familiar to model aircraft enthusiasts, it makes a nicely sized little job and to many a more satisfactory model than the Y2. The plastic seats and fenders have been produced in several shades of brown, so called 'light' or 'dark' seat versions being equally obtainable in different shops at the time of issue. The early 'Schweppes' posters were printed in red, but the later ones were more commonly in black. Later posters were on a yellow ground and involved a change to the upper deck hand rail. Avoid strong sunlight, the upper deck is plastic and will probably fade more readily than the painted lower body.

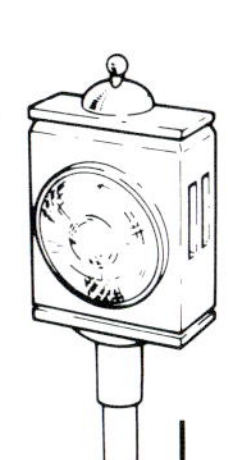

Schweppes   TONIC WATER
GENERAL
HITHER G^EN ST^N
HARROW ROAD
PADDINGTON ST^N
VICTORIA ST^N
CAMBERWELL G^EN
NEW · GATE
LEWISHAM · CATFORD
BEASLEY'S SOAP
BEASLEY'S SOAP

Purveyors to
His Majesty
King George V
SCHWEPPES®
SODA WATER
DRY GINGER ALE
Etc.
GENERAL

Fire Engines

Y4 Shand-Mason Horse-Drawn Fire Engine

To some collectors a model road vehicle is not complete unless accompanied by driver, passengers and where applicable, horses. To others there is something slightly absurd about a stationary item standing on a shelf coupled to a team of trotting horses not getting anywhere, telepathically controlled by a driver without reins. These people prefer unattended, 'parked' motor vehicles in their collections. Old fire engines attract an enthusiastic following and few manufacturers fail to include at least one in their ranges. Yesteryear collectors are fortunate in having two – one in each category – issued some 17 years apart. This, one of the early small-scale models, was first issued in 1960 and bears the date 1905 though somehow one feels that it should be considerably older since it wears such a positively Victorian aspect.

Against this is set the fact that the original was apparently pressed into service during the second world war and is still in working order. There are several guides to the timescale of this model within its production run, the most obvious ones being the markings 'Kent' or later 'London Fire Brigade'. The colour of the horses, white and grey later changed to black and white. Late crew members also had black helmets in place of the highly polished brass ones remembered from pre-war days. Casting differences include the number of rivets securing the horse bar – one, later two – and the design of the boiler mounting including the incorporation of 12, 8 or 7 perforations in the rear platform. Some models may have silver boilers in place of the more usual brass ones.

KENT FIRE BRIGADE
LONDON FIRE BRIGADE
NDON
BRIGADE
72

Y6 1920 Rolls-Royce Fire Engine

Produced from 1977 this rather impressive vehicle is a rare, if not unique, example of a Lesney 'Yesteryear' based on a non-production original – being a thirteen year old Rolls converted for fire-fighting in the early 1930s. As a model this one would grace any collector's shelf. Not a lot of changes since it was introduced which, since there is only the one original, is not surprising, any such being confined to minor casting changes and wheel colours. On a less obvious level the paint used may vary from the lighter to the darker shades of red, though not enough to notice unless examples of each are stood side by side. The black or brown driver and crew seating has been found interchanged in colour, and the later 1983 examples sport white ladders in place of the original brown. The model shares the Y7 Rolls baseplate and this, or both numbers, may be found underneath.

BOROUGH GREEN & DISTRICT

Commercials

Y4 Sentinel Steam Wagon

While not overly common on the roads of this country steam vehicles like this were far from being rare during the 'twenties and even the 'thirties, the commercial world retaining steam as a motive power for rather longer than the private motorist, although steam cars were still being produced elsewhere well into the 1930s. After the war, probably because there were so many war surplus lorries and trucks both available and cheap, a 'steamer' was a novel sight indeed and the last few in general use seem to have faded out by the mid-1950s; road rollers, however, were to remain steam-powered for some time longer. This little 'Sand and Gravel' wagon was part of the original Yesteryear range, produced from 1956. It was always finished in the blue, yellow and red shown, though the precise shades of all three colours may vary. Early models had axles which were clenched at one end, later ones being riveted at both. Even later the previously grey metal wheels were replaced with standard wheels from the '75' series manufactured in black plastic. This model was only produced for about four years, being withdrawn by 1960.

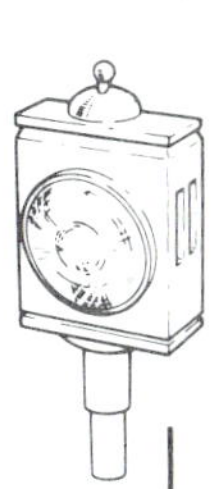

SAND & GRAVEL SUPPLIES
SAND &
GRAVEL SUP

Y6 1916 AEC 'Y' Type Lorry

A rather spartan little model of an equally spartan lorry whose lack of such refinements as windscreen and pneumatic tyres gives it a somewhat archaic look. Similar to the W.D. 'Three-tonner' which saw extensive service during the first world war, this AEC type ceased production in 1921. This means that there were still some of them about in the early 1930s since this was before the concept of 'planned obsolescence' took over and things were expected to last. Produced from 1958 in the small scale utilised for the original Yesteryears this model retained the grey colour scheme and markings shown for the whole of its short production life which had ceased by 1961. The shades of grey may vary from light to dark and a faintly blue/grey is sometimes observed. The intensity of the black outlines to the lettering may also differ and the axles may be clenched or riveted over metal or, infrequently, plastic wheels. This model has a driver installed for those who prefer one. For those who do not, he is painted a similar grey to the cab and is barely noticeable.

Y7 4 Ton Leyland Lorry

Like the AEC Y Type this is another lorry with its roots in the first world war, being a civilianised version of the RFC Heavy Tender. A rather ungainly little model at first sight, but its colouring and markings lend it a charm of its own and the scale of 100:1 means that it can take its place among the greys, blues and reds of the other items from the 1920s London scene. First issued in 1957 the model maintained the same livery throughout its production life, the body being finished in one of several shades of brown including one with a strong maroon cast. The roof may be cream or white, again with several shade differences. Early versions had clenched axles which gave way to the riveted type and the late issues had black plastic wheels in place of the earlier grey metal ones. Like several other early models in the range this lorry had a relatively brief production life by current Yesteryear standards, being withdrawn by 1961.

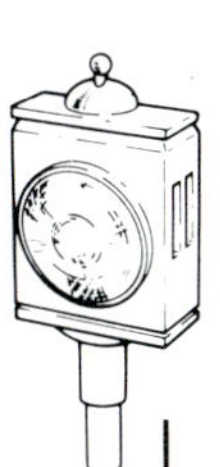

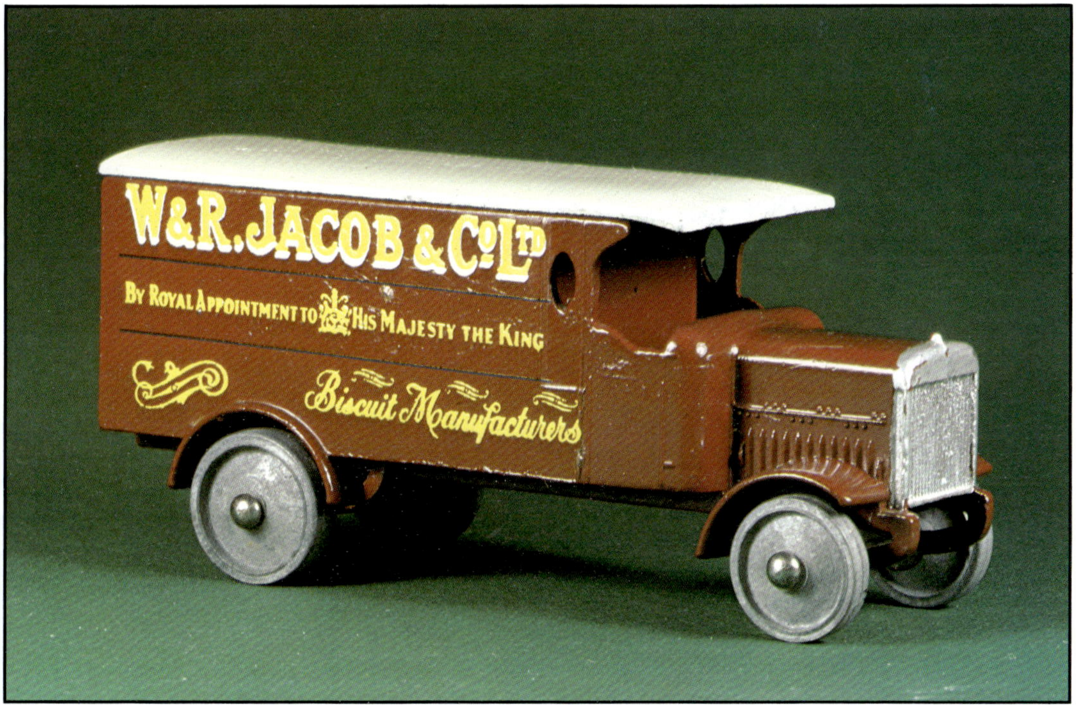
W&R. JACOB & Co. Ltd
By Royal Appointment to His Majesty the King
Biscuit Manufacturers

Y3 1912 Ford 'T' Tanker

Representing one of the smaller tankers which these days are more usually associated with the delivery of paraffin rather than petrol this model utilising the Y12 Ford 'T' baseplate with the Y12 blanked out, appeared in BP livery late in 1981 when the catalogued Y3 was still the Riley MPH. Most people seeing the new tanker for the first time seemed to be quite taken with it, certainly the colour combination of green, red, white and gold works well. Some excitement was generated when it was found that the tankers included in the new Gift Set, the first for some years, were devoid of the black shading under the 'BP' on the tank, but in the event unshaded models also appeared on the stockists' shelves individually packed. The 'Zerolene' tanker was reputedly aimed at the Continental market and some certainly arrived there though a few batches of them seem to have been sold in the UK in 1982 before they were discovered to be not on general sale and became a 'limited edition' with a price tag to match. The 'Express Dairies' issue of 1983 was on general release although the BP version remained the catalogued tanker for that year.

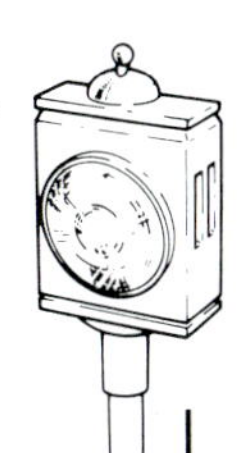

MOTOR "B P" SPIRIT
MOTOR "B P" SPIRIT
"BP"
"BP"
2603
BRITISH PETROLEUM
COMPANY LTD
12 MPH

STANDARD OIL COMPANY
ZEROLENE
STANDARD OIL FOR
MOTOR CARS
No 7
STANDARD
OIL
COMPANY

EXPRESS DAIRY
EXPRESS
DAIRY
BRANCHES
ALL OVER
LONDON
163
EST. 1864
12 MPH

Y5 1927 Talbot Van

The first of the vans and also the first of the new generation 'commercials' after a long break, the very pretty 'Lipton's Tea' van with its opening rear doors generated some excitement when it was issued in 1978. Five years, six more colour schemes and at least three variations later it still remains quite popular. The Royal Crest on the first ones was superseded fairly early on by a company logo, supposedly because permission to use it had not been obtained. The 'Chocolat Menier' and 'Taystee Bread' versions were aimed at markets in France and the US respectively, the latter initially as a product promotional model, before both were catalogued for general release. The Taystee Bread model may be found with a yellow or, less frequently a black baseplate. The 'Nestles' issue arrived in and disappeared from the shops fairly rapidly late in 1981. A light grey roofed variant was available, sometimes being described as the Australian issue, though the darker grey roofs vary in shade quite considerably anyway. The next catalogued one was the 'Chivers' van which appeared about mid-1982, while the 'Wright's Coal Tar Soap' version just made it by Christmas of that year. This may be found with both brass and chrome brightwork. The latest to emerge by the end of 1983 was the 'Ever Ready' van which may have black or fawn seats, while the catalogued one remained the 'Chivers' model. This Yesteryear is reputed to be based on a Talbot chassis which was never actually used for commercial vans, but is thought to have been fitted with ambulance, hearse or 'Black Maria' bodies.

LIPTON'S
TEA
LIPTON'S
TEA
CITY ROAD, LONDON, E.C.1

CHOCOLAT
Menier

Taystee
OLD FASHIONED
ENRICHED BREAD
Taystee
OLD FASHIONED
ENRICHED BREAD

NESTLE'S
MILK
The Richest in Cream

CHIVERS
&
SONS LTD
Jams, Jellies, & Marmalades
THE ORCHARD FACTORY
HISTON
CAMBRIDGE

Wright's
Wright's
Wright Layman & Umney Ltd.

EverReady
BATTERIES for life !

Y12 1912 Ford Model 'T' Van

Another one of the 'who'd have thought it' models this time a perfectly nice little Ford T van complementing, though to a slightly larger scale, the existing Talbot van introduced the previous year. Only the second of the 'new generation' commercials it was originally issued in 1979 as the 'Colman's Mustard' van, with the 'Coca-Cola' and 'Suze Gentiane' variants for the US and French markets, the latter becoming a general release shortly after.

Before going into too much detail about the different liveries worn by this model, one or two basic points regarding age and sequence should be established. The original rear doors on early issues of the model were of a printed-on, single-line type. These gave way to a double-line printed version with decorative hinges early in 1982, and to the current engraved type in 1983. Several vans may carry more than one door type, though none will carry those of a pattern earlier than the year of their introduction. Thus a 'Colman's' van may have the first or second type, a 'Bird's Custard' the second or third, and a Royal Mail only the latest. To this situation may be added the complication that the double doors on the yellow vans can be found printed in black or red. An additional feature, the adoption of the Y12 baseplate for the Y3 tanker subsequent to which the Y12 was removed from the now common casting, has been mentioned elsewhere.

The other thing that must be said about the Y12 vans is that the chrome or 'brass' plating for the brightwork has been selected to suit each model. Although these Fords are of the brass-radiator era some of the models (such as the 25 Year 'Silver' Anniversary Van) have been enhanced by the use of chrome

COLMAN'S
MUSTARD

Enjoy
Coca-Cola

SUZE
A LA GENTIANE

THE BES
POTATO
SMITHS
CRISPS
17
ALWAYS
READY
FOR ALL
MEALS
58-60
BRINKWAY
STOCKPORT

Cerebos
Table
Salt
SEE HOW IT RUNS!

HARRODS
EXPRESS DELIVERY
MOTOR
ACCESSORIES

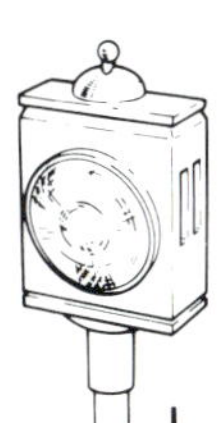

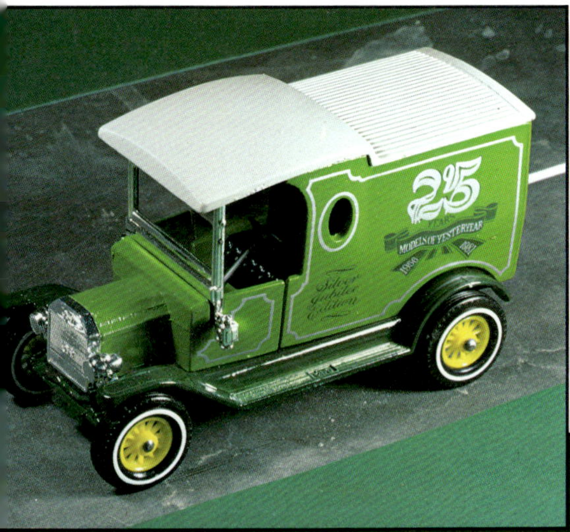
25
MODELS OF YESTERYEAR
Silver Jubilee Edition

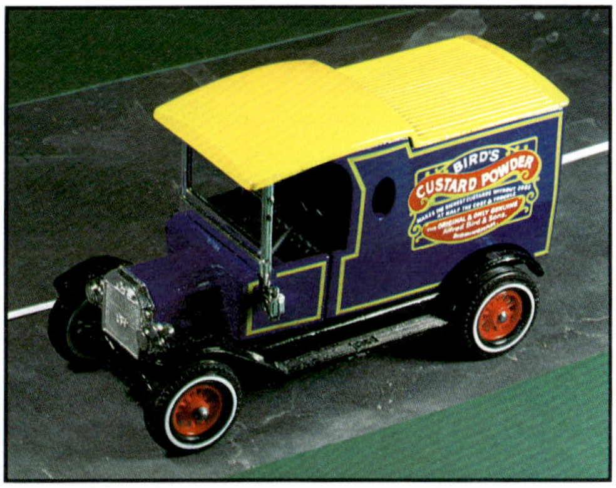
BIRD'S
CUSTARD POWDER

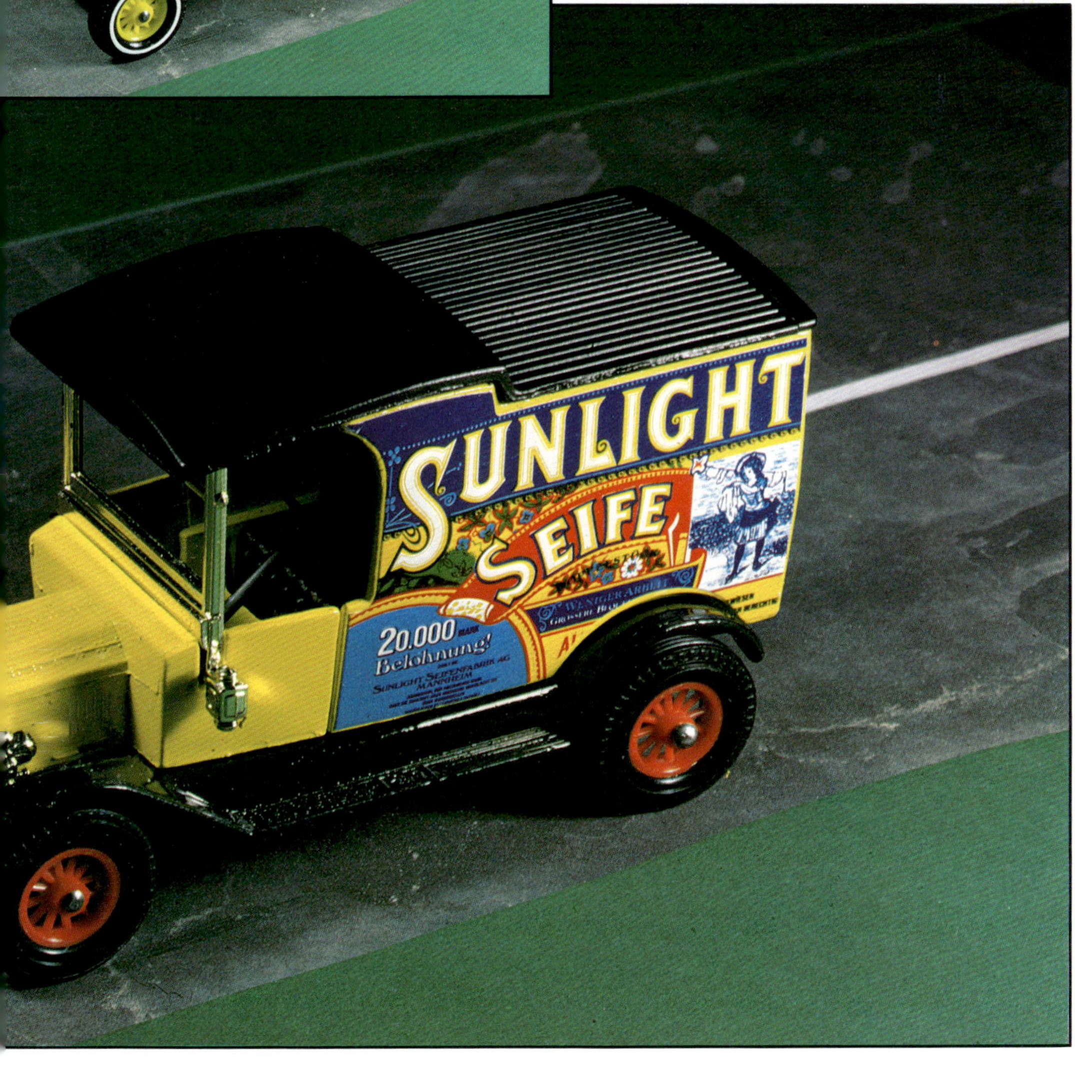
SUNLIGHT
SEIFE
20.000 MARK
Belohnung!
SUNLIGHT SEIFENFABRIK AG MANNHEIM

plating, and the blue, white and silver of the 'Smith's Crisps' van contrasts favourably with the green, beige and 'brass' of the 'Harrod's' model. After the initially issued vans the 'Smith's Crisps' version appeared in 1981, originally offered in exchange for tokens (and cash) collected from Crisps packets though it did reach the shops later for one issue. The 25th Anniversary model was on sale just in time for Christmas of that year. 1982 saw the arrival of the 'Bird's Custard' (catalogued), 'Cerebos Salt', and 'Harrod's' first versions, the latter having black seats and printed doors. 1982 also saw the release of the 'Arnotts Biscuits' van for Australia and the 'Sunlight Seife' one for the Continental markets, the prices originally asked in the UK for these two reflecting the cost of their return fares. 1983 started with a second 'Harrod's' van, this time with black seats and engraved doors, followed by a Royal Mail van the second batch of which are a slightly brighter red than the first batch. The 'Captain Morgan's Rum' van catalogued for 1983 appeared in the Autumn, some fitted with one-piece labels which cracked rather badly across the body joints, others with twin transfers each side which were much neater. The details and letter sizes on the two types are not identical. A third 'Harrod's' was issued at about the same time with tan coloured seats and the last issue for the year, a 'Hoover' van with a special box, was the pre-Christmas release for 1983.

ARNOTT'S
FAMOUS
SAO
BISCUITS
WILLIAM ARNOTT LTD
HOMEBUSH
ROYAL MAIL
GR
Captain 
Morgan
CAPTAIN MORGAN RUM DISTILLERS
DACRE STREET
LONDON SW1
Black
Label 
RUM
The
HOOVER
It BEATS
as it Sweeps
as it Cleans

Y13 1918 Crossley

This model has really enjoyed two leases of life since its introduction in 1974 when Lesneys still thought in terms of one vehicle for each Yesteryear issue. Introduced as the Crossley RAF Tender (frequently referred to as the Ambulance), even the baseplate was marked as such. Quite a neat little model in its own way, it always looked slightly out of place among the brightly coloured cars then forming the bulk of the range with its Service blue-grey body, khaki or less commonly olive-green canvasses and RAF roundel and Red Cross. Some five or six years later it seems as if the potential of this chassis was recognised as a basis for a new commercial vehicle to join the Talbot and Ford vans which had by now found their own following, and so the Evans Coal and Coke lorry emerged. During this model's run the words 'RAF Tender' disappeared from the baseplate which simply became 'Crossley'. In 1983 the model changed yet again, reverting to its earlier canvas top with a new paint scheme as the 'Carlsberg' lorry. This may sometimes be found with silver wheels in place of the more usual brass. The first Carlsbergs carried the original Lesney markings, but the bulk of the production run carry the new marking 'Matchbox Toys Ltd'.

133

Y22 1930 Ford Model 'A' Van

After the introduction of the Ford A chassis with its Woody Wagon body in 1981, few Yesteryear enthusiasts were surprised by the appearance of this little van in the 1982/83 catalogue since the new chassis was such an obvious candidate for another multi-liveried 'commercial'. Perhaps the only surprising thing was that it bore a new Y-number even though the chassis and plastic components right down to the number plate were identical (though of course the tanker had already done the same thing a year earlier). To the collectors, who happily look forward to each new livery on an existing vehicle, this one offered a potential new range, while to those who complain that they collect models not paint and transfers it is perhaps a less happy prospect. Finished in the bright 'OXO' red colour scheme shown here the only variation is the shape of the roof, the rarer ones having an un-textured surface to the top of the driving cab. This was the first Yesteryear to embody glazed windows. Towards the end of 1983 an eagerly awaited issue was the 'Maggi Soup' version, which in the event did not make it by the end of the year.

OXO
IT'S 'MEAT & DRINK' TO YOU
OXO
UBE

Y25 1910 Renault Type AG

The second completely new model among the changed companies and colour schemes catalogued for 1983, the Renault van was as keenly anticipated as the equally new Bugatti. Bearing the livery (not 'advertising' as one authority puts it) of the famous French mineral water, this one is finished in the two-tone green and white eminently consistent with the labels on the bottles. The only thing that really jars is the colour of the seats – that dreadful white plastic which marred so many models and is hardly the ideal seat colour for the conveyance of an overalled crate-humper. Be that as it may, the Type AG was a widely used chassis – the Marne taxi was based on it among others, and one wonders what forms it will take among future Yesteryears.

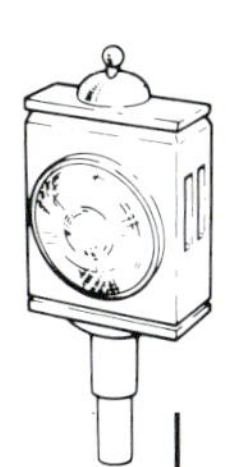

perrier
perrier
MISE EN BOUTEILLE A LA
SOURCE VERGEZE (GARD)
FRANCE

Steam Road Engines

Y1 Allchin 7N HP Steam Traction Engine

Contemplation of the extraordinary prices being asked (and obtained) for the original Yesteryear issues leads one to wonder how these early, simple and in some cases relatively primitive little models came to be so avidly collected. This, the original Y1, has perhaps a more readily understandable appeal than some of the others since steam traction engines seem to generate enormous enthusiasm nowadays if the crowds who flock to Steam Rallies are any guide. This one is quite a dainty little representative of the species in its own right. Originally issued in 1956 it maintained a green and red colour scheme throughout its production life, though the red of the wheels became brighter in colour as time went by and the serrations of the rear wheel rims changed from straight across to angled. The very late ones had plain wheels with no serrations at all. The wheel rims may be painted or plain for the angled versions, unpainted on the others. Early models had the wheels secured with clenched axles. Later axles were riveted at both ends. The boiler door changed in colour from copper, through gold to a silver plated finish.

Y9 Fowler 'Big Lion' Showman's Engine

Probably the most impressive of all the original Yesteryears, the splendid Showman's Engine really made an impact when it was first released in 1958. Even now, viewed from some 25 years later, if its overall appearance and finish are compared with the simplicity of the early lorries and cars among which it first emerged – and which were to continue to much the same standard for some years more – it seems to have come from a different and more expensive range altogether. Indeed, measured against the sophistication of much later Yesteryears it still stands out as a miniature 'classic', long-term familiarity not-withstanding. The model was produced in several shades of brown and red, changing from dark chocolate to a quite pronounced red as time went by. Early roofs were cream, changing to white, though both white and cream roofs may be found on the later, lighter red versions. They however provide less of a guide than the body colour or the smoke box doors which, like those on the Allchin, changed from copper, through gold, to a silver plated finish.

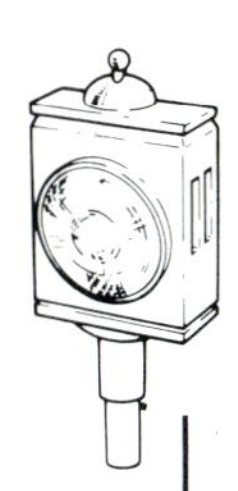

LESNEY'S MODERN AMUSEMENTS

Y11 1920 Aveling & Porter Steam Roller

Another one for the steam enthusiasts, this time a rather nobby little steam roller to go with the two steam traction engines whose scale of 80:1 it shares. Sometimes considered a little less appealing than the other two, but perhaps this is a townsman's view since steam-rollers like this were so common until quite recent years, even if most of them did seem to have Invicta on the front, while traction engines, like the Allchin, tended towards the more rural occupations. It's a pity that the small size of the model precludes the addition of the chains by which the vehicle was steered, but that aside it really is quite a well made little job. First introduced in 1958 and always turned out in the generally if slightly variable green, red and black (sometimes dark brown) colour scheme shown. Some casting differences exist including a slightly lower roof line on the later models, and variations in the depth of the recession of the spokes inside the rollers. Additionally the later ones had a little less gold paint, but broadly speaking they all looked very much like these.

Railway Engines

Y13 American General Locomotive 'Santa Fe'

Lesneys seldom failed to include a railway engine in at least one of their ranges at some time, and the early Yesteryears were no exception. Even without the name on the side this locomotive would be instantly recognised as an early American by any 'movie' fan with an inclination towards 'Westerns'. Its characteristic smoke stack was designed to prevent sparks from the engine setting fire to the passing countryside; a sort of early form of emission control. The large frontal structure was usually described as a 'cow-catcher', though looking more suitable for the bows of an ice-breaker than for the purpose of deflecting bovine obstructions. That said, it's an eye-catching little item, even if like the GWR loco it is singularly devoid of rolling stock. Unfortunately the scale of 112:1 is not compatible with anything else in the set. This one was issued from 1959 in green and maroon, the later versions wearing a lighter shade of green than the original dark colour. At one time the headlamp lens was painted silver though as time went by, the silver disappeared as did some of the quite extensive gold trim on walkways, domes and boiler door, only the smoke stack retaining it to the end.

Y14 GWR Locomotive 'Duke of Connaught'

Non railway enthusiasts are invariably impressed by the reverence accorded the old Great Western Railway by steam train devotees. True there were some very advanced, in some cases revolutionary, innovations introduced by this company particularly under the guidance of that great engineer Isambard Kingdom Brunel. But even now, years after the line lost its individual identity, the magic of the initials GWR would appear to remain. Lesneys, when selecting a companion railway engine for their 'Santa Fe' loco, settled on the 1890s-built 4-2-2- 'Duke of Connaught' which distinguished itself in 1903 with an extremely fast run from Bristol to London. Modelled to a scale of 130:1 this tiny locomotive was issued from 1959 in the green and dark brown shown throughout its production life. Early ones may be identified by the free-running wheels on the axles and the separation of the off-side walkway from the driving wheel casing. As time went by the wheels became fixed to the axles, the walkway and casing were joined, and the gold paint disappeared from several locations. A late version with a silver smoke box door is also rumoured.

Tomorrow's Yesteryears

In basing this guide on the Yesteryear scene from 1956 until 1983, the compilers set specific time limits for the reasons stated in Chapter 1, taking the view that this was a clearly identifiable time span in the Yesteryear collector's world.

What does the future hold for the Yesteryear enthusiast? What, if any, will be Tomorrow's Yesteryears?

Reviewing the new models released in 1983 – the Type 44 Bugatti and the Renault van – the impression is gained that although these were produced under the banner of Matchbox Toys, they still bore the characteristics of the earlier models in the series. The delicacy of line displayed by the Bugatti was eminently consistent with those models, as was the marked 'family resemblance' borne by the Renault. The remaining releases for 1983 were vehicles which had become familiar under the Lesney Industries label in previous years.

It must also be said that, at its best, the general finish of these was as good as ever.

The first noticeable thing about the 1984 season releases was the introduction of a new box, somewhat simpler in design than the 'Straw' box it supersedes. It reverts to a non-transparent back (unfortunately preventing the contents from being inspected from both sides) and is coloured a brownish red, with lighter red edges and detail. A non-removable internal

148

restraint, lustre finished in a light coffee colour, shows off the model to advantage and makes it easier to remove.

The line-up of new releases for this and subsequent years has remained very much 'the mixture as before', involving new colour schemes and altered liveries for the existing models (now issued under new 'Y' numbers). These were to include a small, but steady stream of completely new models, initially rather square in their general shape. It was these latter from the Y27 Foden onwards which seemed to indicate the end of the Lesney design influence most clearly. They have included:

Y27 1922 Foden Steam Lorry. Nicely turned out in blue and red with a grey canvas top and bearing Pickford's markings. Quite an eye-catching item, fitted with very realistic solid-tyred wheels newly-crafted for the model. The prototype, shown at one of the more prestigious Swapmeets in the south of England, looked a bit 'chunky' at first sight, but in the event the version reaching the shops has fast become a firm favourite. Steam enthusiasts however, have criticised the all-brass smoke-stack which should, more properly, be brass-tipped black and they also highlighted the fact that the rear wheels of this period should be larger and more substantial than the front ones. (Later on Fodens looking very like this were to be fitted with disc wheels and pneumatic tyres and yes, the rear wheels on these were larger too).

Y28 1907 Unic Taxi. The pre-First World War Barnes-based taxicab. A model greeted with horror and consternation, described as a caricature or a Disneyland prop. The expression 'Happy Cab' was also bandied about. The prototype of this taxi was not much liked when it was also shown at the same Swapmeet. To their credit, Matchbox Toys took that opportunity to meet and talk to their collectors.

Whether this had any influence or not, the model which finally emerged on to the market was considerably more acceptable, only the small diameter, thick-tyred wheels introducing a jarring note.

Y29 1919 Walker Electric Van. At one time a familiar sight on the streets of London these 3^{1}/$_{2}$ HP Harrods vans were in use from the early '20s until they, or something very much like them, faded out in the middle 1960s. This model, the third of the new Matchbox Toys Yesteryears to be released, displays an attention to detail in design quality and paintwork which is quite extraordinary, the former being exemplified by such things as the detailed panelling behind the driver's seat, the latter by the decoration on the front elevation. This was the first Yesteryear not bearing a scale on the box, and like the earlier Y12 Harrod's vans was initially only available from Brompton Road.

The most exciting thing about the 1984 programme was the introduction of the 'Connoisseur's Collection', a hand-made wooden case containing a set of six models comprising 1964 Y1 Ford T, 1966 Y3 Benz, 1967 Y4 Opel, 1964 Y11 Packard, 1966 Y13 Daimler and 1965 Y14 Maxwell, each fitted with their original type wheels and beautifully finished in special colour schemes complete with coach-lines where these apply. It was this quite outstanding production, more than anything else, which really recognised the change of emphasis from 'Toys for Children' to 'Collector's Models' for which quite large sums of money could change hands, a phenomenon which had become increasingly apparent during the period reviewed in the guide.

Additional evidence of this may be seen in the increasingly frequent release of models issued as Limited Editions – and packed in boxes so marked – produced in relatively small numbers, though in

quantities less absurd than the Collector's Club specials. With some reservations this could prove to be good news for present collectors, bad news for future collectors – and no news at all for the youngsters at whom the whole thing was originally aimed.

These factors, coupled with the continuing improvements in casting and detail design evident in the latest prototypes to be shown – the newer models losing the slightly clumsy look of those first Matchbox Toys offerings – would suggest that providing the market is not overwhelmed with multi-liveried Special Edition commercials, the future for the Yesteryear collector is in good hands for as long as the makers can maintain the quality they are now establishing.

In this we wish them well.

Appendix 'A'

Yesteryear scales vary considerably. This Appendix lists the scales shown in the catalogues or on the boxes between 1956 and 1983 and the models within each scale, though in fact some of the scales quoted are suspect as described in the text. The Appendix sequences the identifying Y Number for each model by the initial date of issue of that model.

34:1	Sunbeam Motor Cycle	1962 (Y8)
35:1	1912 Ford 'T' Tanker	1981 (Y3)
	1912 Ford 'T' Vans	1979 (Y12)
	1934 Riley	1974 (Y3)
	1937 Cord	1979 (Y18)
	1945 MG	1978 (Y8)
38:1	1909 Opel	1967 (Y4)
	1910 Renault Van	1983 (Y25)
	1924 Bugatti	1983 (Y24)
	1936 SS100	1977 (Y1)
40:1	1911 Renault	1963 (Y2)
	1930 Ford 'A'	1981 (Y21)
42:1	1911 Ford 'T'	1964 (Y1)
	1935 Auburn	1980 (Y19)
43:1	1907 Peugeot	1969 (Y5)
	1930 Duesenberg	1976 (Y4)
	1938 Lagonda	1972 (Y11)
44:1	1931 Stutz*	1974 (Y14)
45:1	1904 Spyker	1961 (Y16)
	1911 Daimler	1966 (Y13)
	1928 Mercedes-Benz	1972 (Y16)
	1937 Mercedes-Benz	1981 (Y20)

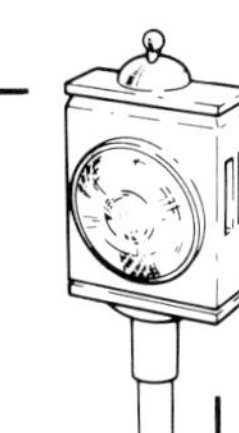

46:1	1913 Mercer	1961 (Y7)
	1930 Packard	1969 (Y15)
47:1	1914 Vauxhall	1970 (Y2)
	1918 Crossley	1974 (Y13)
	1927 Talbot Vans	1978 (Y5)
48:1	1909 Thomas	1967 (Y12)
	1912 Simplex	1968 (Y9)
	1912 Rolls-Royce	1968 (Y7)
	1913 Cadillac	1967 (Y6)
	1914 Stutz	1969 (Y8)
	1920 Rolls-Royce	1977 (Y6)
	1923 Bugatti	1961 (Y6)
	1938 Hispano-Suiza	1975 (Y17)
49:1	1911 Maxwell	1965 (Y14)
50:1	1921 Packard	1964 (Y11)
	1928 Morris	1958 (Y8)
51:1	1906 Rolls-Royce	1969 (Y10)
52:1	1929 Bentley	1962 (Y5)
	1928 Mercedes-Benz	1963 (Y10)
54:1	1908 Mercedes	1958 (Y10)
	1910 Benz	1966 (Y3)
55:1	1906 Rolls-Royce	1960 (Y15)
	1929 Bentley	1958 (Y5)
63:1	1905 Shand Mason	1960 (Y4)
72:1	1922 AEC 'S'	1983 (Y23)
80:1	Allchin	1956 (Y1)
	Aveling and Porter	1958 (Y11)
	1924 Fowler	1958 (Y9)
100:1	1918 Sentinel	1956 (Y4)
	1916 AEC 'Y'	1958 (Y6)
	Leyland	1957 (Y7)
	1899 Horse Bus	1959 (Y12)
	1911 AEC 'B' Bus	1956 (Y2)
112:1	1862 4-4-0 Loco	1959 (Y13)
130:1	1907 'E' Type Tram	1956 (Y3)
	1897 GWR Loco	1959 (Y14)

*43$^1/_2$:1 on some boxes

Index

			Box	Page
	'A & J Box'		ST	
	'OXO' Van	Y22	ST	134
Ford Model 'T' (1911)	Red/Black	Y1	MB/WB	26
	White/Red		WG	
Ford Model 'T' Tanker (1912)	'BP'	Y3	ST	122
	'Express Dairies'		ST	
	'Zerolene'		ST	
Ford Model 'T' Van (1912)	'Arnotts'	Y12	ST	126
	'Birds'		ST	
	'Capt. Morgans'		ST	
	'Cerebos'		ST	
	'Coca Cola'		ST	
	'Colmans'		ST	
	'Harrods'		Spec	
	'Hoover'		Spec	
	'Royal Mail'		ST	
	'Smith's Crisps'		ST	
	'Sunlight Seife'		ST	
	'Suze'		ST	
	25 Year Anniversary		Spec	
Fowler 'Big Lion' Showmans Engine		Y9	MB	140

H

			Box	Page
Hispano-Suiza Type K.6 (1938)	Metallic Red/Black	Y17	WG	90
	Blue/Blue		ST	
	Blue/Black		ST	

L

			Box	Page
Lagonda D'Head Coupe (1938)	Gold/Purple	Y11	WB	72
	Metallic Orange/Bronze		WG	
	Beige/Black		ST	
Leyland 4 Ton Lorry 'Jacobs'		Y7	MB	120
Locomotive, American General 'Sante Fe' (1862)		Y13	MB	144
Locomotive, GWR 'Duke of Connaught' (1903)		Y14	MB	146

M

			Box	Page
Maxwell Roadster Model GA (1911)		Y14	MB/WB	78
Mercedes-Benz SS Coupe (1928)	Silver/Metallic Red	Y16	WB	88
	Metallic Green		WG	
	White/Black		ST	
	Blue/Grey		ST	
Mercedes-Benz 36/220 (1928)		Y10	MB/WB	66
Mercedes-Benz 540K (1938)		Y20	ST	96
Mercedes GP (1908)		Y10	MB	64
Mercer Raceabout (1913)	Lilac	Y7	MB	52
	Yellow		MB	

	Colour		Box	Page
MG TC (1945)	Green	Y8	ST	60
	Red		ST	
	Blue		ST	
Morris 'Cowley' Bullnose (1926)		Y8	MB	56

O

	Colour		Box	Page
Opel Coupe (1909)	White	Y4	MB	38
	Orange/Black		WG	

P

	Colour		Box	Page
Packard Landaulette (1912)		Y11	MB/WB	70
Packard Victoria (1930)	Metallic Bronze/Brown	Y15	WB	84
	Metallic Yellow/Black		WG	
	Red/Black		ST	
Peugeot (1907)	Yellow/Black	Y5	WB	46
	Gold/Black		WG	

R

	Colour		Box	Page
Renault Two-Seater (1911)		Y2	MB/WB	30
Renault Type AG Van 'Perrier' (1910)		Y25	ST	136
Riley MPH (1934)	Metallic Red		WG	36
	Blue	Y3	ST	
Rolls-Royce Fire Engine (1920)		Y6	WG/ST	114
Rolls-Royce (Landaulette) (1912)	Silver/Red	Y7	MB	54
	Silver/Metallic Grey		WB	
	Gold/Red		WG	
	Yellow/Black		ST	
Rolls-Royce 'Silver Ghost' (1906)	Metallic Lime/Grey	Y10	WB	68
	White/Metallic/Red		WG	
	Silver		ST	
Rolls-Royce 'Silver Ghost' (1907)		Y15	MB/WB	82

S

	Colour		Box	Page
Sentinel Steam Wagon 'Sand & Gravel'		Y4	MB	116
Shand Mason Fire Engine (1905)		Y4	MB	112
Simplex Model 50 (1912)	Green	Y9	MB	62
	Gold/Metallic Red		WB	
	Red/Black		WG	
	Red/Black/Yellow		ST	
Spyker (1904)		Y16	MB/WB	86
SS100 Jaguar (1936)	White	Y1	WG	28

			Box	Page
	Metallic Blue		ST	
	Green		ST	
Stutz 'Bearcat' (1931)	Metallic Green	Y14	WG	80
	Red/Cream		ST	
	Cream/Green		ST	
Stutz Type 4E Roadster (1914)	Metallic Red	Y8	WB	58
	Metallic Blue		WG	
Sunbeam M/c & Sidecar (1914)		Y8	MB/WB	102

T

			Box	Page
Talbot Van (1927)	'Chivers'	Y5	ST	124
	'Ever Ready'		ST	
	'Liptons'		WG/ST	
	'Choc. Menier'		WG/ST	
	'Nestles'		ST	
	'Taystee Bread'		ST	
	'Wrights'		ST	
Thomas 'K' 6-70 (1909)	Metallic Blue	Y12	MB/WB	74
	Metallic Red		WG	
Tramcar, London 'E' Class (1907)		Y3	MB	106

V

			Box	Page
Vauxhall 'Prince Henry' (1914)	Red/Silver	Y12	WB	32
	Metallic Blue		WG	
	Red/Silver Black		ST